# PARADISE POEMS

# Gerald Stern

# PARADISE
# POEMS

Vintage Books

A Division of Random House
New York

FIRST VINTAGE BOOKS EDITION, September 1984

Portions of this work have previously appeared in the following publications:
*American Poetry Review, Antaeus, The Black Warrior Review, Columbia,*
*Crazy Horse, Fiction International, Field, The Georgia Review, MSS,*
*Nation, The New Yorker, Ohio Review, Paris Review,*
*Poesis, Poetry* and *Sonora Review.*

The poems "Baja" and "Villa-Lobos" have previously appeared in the book
*On Equal Terms,* published by The Symposium Press.

Library of Congress Cataloging in Publication Data

Stern, Gerald.
Paradise poems.

I. Title.
PS3569.T3888P37   1984b     811'.54     84-40053
ISBN 0-394-72619-7 (pbk.)

*Manufactured in the United States of America*

# Contents

# PARADISE POEMS

# ORANGE ROSES

I am letting two old roses stand for everything I believe in.
I am restricting the size of the world, keeping it inside that plastic pot.
This is like Greece, the roses sitting in the hot sun,
the leaves exhausted,
the blue sky surrounding them.

I reach my fingers inside the dirt
and slowly scrape the sides.
One more flower will bloom the rest of this month,
probably symbolizing the last breath left
after a lifetime of tearful singing.

The wall in back of me is no part of this.
It shows only a large shadow overcome with thought.
It shows him in ruins,
his body spread out in all directions,
his pencil uprooted, his own orange roses dark and hidden.

# LATER TODAY

Later today, when most of the ice is melted
and the water is black again, we'll sit for one minute
on the side porch and stare at the bright shadows.
We'll start talking about the wall
and the green pool beside the copper feeder
and how the birch could grow again
and how the door would look with roses on it.
We will live in the light
as if we were still in France,
as if the boats were there
and we were staring into space,
as if we were in Babylon,
walking beside the iron giants,
touching their black beards,
looking at their huge eyes,
going down to our clay houses and our tiny cafés
on the muddy river.

# RHODODENDRON

Here I am again with one more flower,
more lavender than pink this time,
more rich and red than ever.
Here I am after walking back and forth through the grass
with an armful of straw
and a fistful of white dust.
—I bend down to drink
like a lover, my words half muffled
by the bird clack, my secret softened
by the light rain and the dark sunshine.
I smooth the leaves and pull the petals out
with that quick underhand motion.
I prepare for life or death by lying down
with my left arm under my head, by saying my last
words to the two trees, by closing my eyes
to everything else, the dirty woods, the river,
the green tomatoes, the yellow marigolds,
the bloody squirrel, the bitter universe.

# PICKING THE ROSES

I am picking the roses for next time,
Little Darlings for the side of the house,
Tiffany and Lilli Marlene for the hot slope
where the strawberries used to be.
I am doing this in early February
before the ice cracks and the island gets back its dignity.
There is a towel against the front door
to keep the wind out
and newspapers squeezed into the holes
so we can have good reading for the bright wasps.
If there is a boar, he is outside snorting.
We will need him for the bleeding and regeneration to come.

Soon the dead plants will arrive by mail,
the roses in corrugated paper, their roots packed
in excelsior and moss,
the lilies in plastic bags, *their* roots like radishes,
a leaf or two to signify the good life of the future.
When the time comes I will walk outside to hear my name
ring through the trees, or stop for a minute to hear the words skip
on the water or collect like mice behind the garbage cans.
I will tear the ground with my shovel
and bark with pain as I bend down over the roots
and get ready for the dirty water and the dust.

Then for two blocks up and two blocks down
my screams, and the screams of the boar,
will mix together.
There will be talking afterwards and sobbing
and touches of cynicism and histrionics
in the living rooms by the river,
and single voices wailing in the tradition
of the old Orient, and choruses of flies
boring everybody with their small details,
crash of bone against bone,
mixture of broken weapons and falling shadows.

I will clean up
like a ghost at my own funeral.
My poor left eye will be closed shut

behind its puffy hill
and my right thigh will be permanently twisted.
I will sleep my sleep
on top of the mohair sofa,
over the *Inquirer* and the white espresso.
In one month
the twigs will be shining
and I will be rocking in my metal chair
or sitting on my swing
in the little room on the side porch.
One arm I'll hold up in the snake position
above my head
and one arm I'll hold out like a hairy fox
waiting to spring.
I will collect all the stupidity and sorrow
of the universe in one place
and wait—like everyone else—
for the first good signs,
the stems to turn green,
the buds to swell and redden,
the clouds to fall, the trees to bend,
the tenors of all 3,000 counties
to tremble in the grass,
to beat their chests, to tear their shirts,
to stumble against the sopranos, to rise and fall
like birds in the muddy grass,
like heavy birds in last year's muddy grass.

# CLAY DOG

I'll never forget the small red dog in Mexico,
his two long ears and his bulging eyes.
All the passion and courtesy of the artist
are in that body
and all the sweetness of his race.
—I think of him, after a long nap with his wife,
staring up at the sky, and I think of his left hand
resting under her head while his right hand works
above the smoke. I think of him touching her cheek
before he goes back to the sand, maybe toying
all the way down with either a snarling lower lip
or drooping cougar shoulder, maybe putting
a corn cob in the mouth so the teeth will show,
maybe turning the face back like a horse's
or stiffening the legs or flattening the back
to build the tension up in front,
maybe dividing the head into lobes or raising
the nose to give a look of fear or disdain,
maybe scraping the skin until it shines
or adding a little white to the tiny nails—
getting him ready to live under the stars,
letting him join the others,
taking the leaves off, cooling the hot bricks,
saving him from the mud, saving him from the rain,
saving him from the fire.

# IN MEMORY OF W. H. AUDEN

I am going over my early rages again,
my first laments and ecstasies,
my old indictments and spiritualities.
I am standing, like Schiller, in front of Auden's door
waiting for his carved face to let me in.
In my hand is *The Poem of My Heart* I dragged
from one ruined continent to the other,
all my feelings slipping out on the sidewalk.
It was warm and hopeful in his small cave
waiting for the right word to descend
but it was cold and brutal outside on Fourth Street
as I walked back to the Seventh Avenue subway,
knowing, as I reached the crowded stairway,
that I would have to wait for ten more years
or maybe twenty more years for the first riches
to come my way, and knowing that the stick
of that old Prospero would never rest
on my poor head, dear as he was with his robes
and his books of magic, good and wise as he was
in his wrinkled suit and his battered slippers.
—Oh good and wise, but not enough to comfort me,
so loving was he with his other souls.
I had to wait like clumsy Caliban,
a sucker for every vagueness and degeneration.
I had to find my own way back, I had to
free myself, I had to find my own pleasure
in my own sweet cave, with my own sweet music.
   Once a year, later even once a month,
I stood on the shores of Bleecker and Horatio
waving goodbye to that ship all tight and yare
and that great wizard, bobbing up and down
like a dreaming sailor out there, disappearing
just as he came, only this time his face more weary
and his spirit more grave than when he first arrived
to take us prisoner on our own small island,
that poet I now could talk to, that wrinkled priest
whose neck I'd hang on, that magician
who could release me now, whom I release and remember.

# STEVE DUNN'S SPIDER

Down in the sweet pepper bushes,
down in the birches,
down by the manmade lake,
I walk across the causeway
avoiding Steve Dunn's spider,
the little recluse with the white violin on its back.

Down on the nudist's log,
down in the soggy water,
down by the fat girl's tried and true paradise,
I avoid the thin white threads
at any cost,
the week in bed,
the oozing ankle,
the convulsive tightening in the throat,
the year of remorse and burning tissue.

In the twenty-fourth circle,
in the twenty-fourth or twenty-fifth circle,
in the pool of warm blood,
in old *Pomona Real,*
I try to save myself,
I hold the slippery tree between my legs,
I talk to this or that Frenchman,
I talk to a sodomist,
I get ready for earthly bliss,
I go to the furthest limit,
I sink down of my own free will,
I lie on the wavy rocks

and I rise up,
one more time in the brilliant sunlight,
across from the pine trees,
across from the cedars,
king of the water,
lord of the greasy log,
lord of the lake.

# ROMANIA, ROMANIA

I stand like some country crow across the street
from the Romanian Synagogue on Rivington Street
singing songs about Moldavia and Bukovina.
I am a walking violin, screeching
a little at the heights, vibrating a little
at the depths, plucking sadly on my rubber guts.
It's only music that saves me. Otherwise
I would be keeping the skulls forever, otherwise
I would be pulling red feathers from my bloody neck.
It's only music, otherwise I would be white
with anger or giving in to hatred
or turning back to logic and religion—
the Brahms Concerto, hills and valleys of gold,
the mighty Kreutzer, rubies piled over rubies,
a little Bartók, a little ancient Bach—
but more for the thin white tablecloths under the trees
than for Goga and his Christians,
and more for the red petticoats and the cold wine and the garlic
than the railroad station and the submachine guns,
and more for the little turn on Orchard Street
and the life of sweetness and more for the godly Spanish
and the godly Chinese lined up for morning prayers,
and much much more for the leather jackets on sticks
and the quiet smoke
and the plush fire escapes,
and much much more for the silk scarves in the windows
and the cars in the streets
and the dirty invisible stars—
Yehudi Menuhin
wandering through the hemlocks,
Jascha Heifetz
bending down over the tables,
the great Stern himself
dragging his heart from one ruined soul to another.

# IT'S NICE TO THINK OF TEARS

It's nice to think of tears as polliwogs
rolling down your face,
lost on the cheekbones and the distant chin
before they drop on the oilcloth and the pine floor.

It's nice to think of you reaching your hand up
and wiping them away,
all that sadness
welling up, then disappearing.

It's just fantastic to think of sorrow
as water,
to think of it dripping through the leaves
or escaping in the sand,

to see it stretching from one salt island
to another,
or filling the cellar up
and the pools and ditches—

all that grief
where the eyes were,
all that sobbing
where the heart was,

all those rivers flowing
where the swelling had been,
and all those lakes and oceans
where the head was lying,

where the mouth was open,
where the shoulders were bent,
where the hands were hanging down,
where the dark old hands were helpless and hanging down.

# SOULS FROM EMERSON

*For Myrna Smith*

This is a kind of sunflower,
only smaller and less demanding,
on a side street in Phillipsburg
faced away from the truck fumes and the air horns.

It replaces the dead beehives and tobacco leaves,
bowed over from exhaustion,
and crawls over the side of the bird house and the wire fence
like a morning glory or daisy.

I come back here twice,
once to climb the hill
and once to touch the old head
and break a leaf off at the stem.

And I come back to see if I can find
the whitewashed wall
and hear the wild dog again
and see his fenced-in garden, the souls outside

going up and down like souls from Emerson,
trying to find a home on Marshall Street
beside the clothes pins and the oil drum,
near the slush and the pink mimosa—

left on the Parkway just before Jacob's Auto Parts,
across from the green island separating
the cars rushing west to Cleveland and Ypsilanti
and the cars rushing east to Whitehouse and Coney Island.

# SONG

There's nothing in this gardenous world more delightful
than blossoms lying where they fall,
soldiers sprawled from one ravine to another,
lovers under a bloody window.

I look up through the branches
dreaming of fate.
My old enemy the blue sky is above me.
My old enemy the hawk
is moving slowly through the string of white clouds.

One day I will wake up at dawn
and philosophize about my state
as I get ready.
I will put on my heavy shirt
and think of the long and bitter day ahead.

It will take hours to know
whether I will live or die,
which car to get ready,
which woods to pass by,
which animal to ride over,
which bridge to cross on the way.

I love the sight of me
rolled over on the ground.
I love being pierced through the heart,
half a man, half a flower,
reaching my hand out, turning my palm away,
one of the many pink and white blossoms,
one of the many on the brutal lawn.

# WEEPING AND WAILING

I like the way my little harp makes trees
leap, how putting the metal between my teeth
makes half the animals in my backyard quiver,
how plucking the sweet tongue makes the stars
live together in love and ecstasy.

I bend my face and cock my head. My eyes
are open wide listening to the sound.
My hand goes up and down like a hummingbird.
My mouth is opening and closing, I am singing
in harmony, I am weeping and wailing.

# HIDDEN JUSTICE

This is my forest now, this Christmas cactus,
stretching out leaf after leaf,
pink blossom after pink blossom.
This is where I'll go to breathe
and live in darkness
and sit like a frog, and sit like a salamander,
and this is where I'll find a tiny light
and have my vision
and start my school—
in this dry and airy place
beside these trunks
in this fragrant mixture.

I will put my small stage here
under a thick leaf
and I will eat and sleep and preach right here
and put my two dogs there
to keep my two guards busy
with prayer and feeding.
I will live completely for the flowering,
my neck like a swan's,
my fingers clawing the air
looking for justice;
year after year the same,
my fingers clawing the air for hidden justice.

# CHRISTMAS STICKS

Before I leave I'll put two sticks on the porch
so they can talk to each other about poor Poland
and wrap themselves around each other the way sticks
do when most of life is gone. They will lie
a little about Walesa, one will dance
and shake his dried-out leaves as if to threaten
the other, one will lean against the wall
as if there were boots to give him courage, as if
there was a moustache somewhere there among the scars
and a thin sword and a thin tear. I'd make them flower
again, I'd make them drive through Warsaw
on the back of trucks, I'd have them reach their wooden
hands through the flimsy slats and take the gifts
and live out the dream of 1830 and the dream
of 1863, the Russians gone,
the Germans gone, the life remade, the flags
flying over the factories, workers dancing
above the trees, a wedding under a walnut,
the food amazing, the last memory the bride's
father in white showing his empty pockets,
his beard a little white to match his suit,
his eyes all wet, his shirt half open—
all that sweetness, all that golden fat—
the fat I love, the sweetness I love—and the two of them
walking home at night after the wedding
talking to each other again about Pulaski
and Casimir the Great and Copernicus
and what it could have been if only sticks
had ruled the vicious world, remembering again
the Jews arriving from Spain, the scholars of Europe
descending on Cracow, half the Italian painters
living in Poland, the gentry reading books,
the women drawing and playing flutes—
forgetting the dream-crushers out there in the swamps,
forgetting the liars, forgetting the murderers—
two sticks in the moonlight carrying on
after the wedding, lifting their empty bottles
for the last time, one of them heaving his over
a sycamore—a buttonwood tree—one of them
heaving his across a frozen river

and listening with his hands on his bent knees
for the old crash, slow in coming, the impact
a half a minute later than he expected,
both of them laughing at the stupidity,
both of them weeping for the huge carp
frozen in mud, and both of them toasting the bride
with broken hands, with nothing this time, with fingers
ruined and shredded, kissing the dear one goodbye
before they go off like wounded soldiers, home
from fighting the Turks at Vienna, home from fighting
the Deutschers a hundred times and the Rooskies two hundred,
home from fighting the Swedes and the Austrians,
two great masters of suffering and sadness
singing songs about love and regeneration.

# THE SAME MOON ABOVE US

When I see a man sleeping over the grilles
trying to get some heat for his poor stomach
then I think he must be Ovid dreaming
again of Rome, getting ready to write
another letter to Caesar, his third that day,
his tenth or eleventh that week, keeping track
somewhere in those dirty sweaters and coats
of what they owe him now that his labor is over,
now that he's lying there with his hands all grimy
and his face all ruined—

Although I think he is sometimes caught by the horror
as if he had just come to, as if he could finally
let the bitterness take over and just sit there
with his coats wrapped around him, his stinking animal skins
dragging through ice and mud, his mind and body
finally alike, the pedant's dream come true,
the mystic's dream, the lover's dream, his brain
reduced to pulp, his heart surrounded,
his only desire a little warmth, a fire
for his poor fingers, a fire for his poor toes—

I think in his fifties he learned a new language
to go with the freezing rain; he would have done this
anyhow, he would have shouldered his riches
and stripped things down the way men in their fifties
do, only this way he found it easy,
he only had to lift his cold face
from his thin notebook, he only had to look
at the street full of garbage and there he was.
He did have to find another instrument
since flutes wouldn't do and reeds wouldn't do
and the rattle of pencils on the metal grates
wouldn't do—

I see him lying there watching the wind cleaning
the blue sky, pulling a piece of sock
over his raw ankle, asking himself
what he was punished for. Was it because
he sang too much? Was it because

he was too playful, too pathetic? No one could possibly
know him here in New York City outside
the Prince Hotel and the twenty-eight marble steps;
no one could see him with his paper cup
staring up at the dirty ceiling,
trying to remember Love's reception, the white
horses waiting for him, the golden plates
with purple dolphins on them, all that happiness
the one time in his life—

What he thinks he can do sometimes is find
a way to live in this world without rotting
from too much thought, and he thinks he can sometimes walk
past the galvanized soil pipe or the Sid Vicious sign
or even sit all night in his plastic chair
across from the amazing brass ash tray
without half dying; and he thinks he can be an eagle again
and talk to Caesar, and he thinks sometimes, if he's lucky,
he can have his muse back and eat
from her sweet fingers just as he did before
and listen to her song against his lips
as if he were holding the sea in his black hands,
as if, after first giving him all that power,
she now could give him pity and consolation,
now that he's living in horror,
now that his hair is white and his feet are frozen,
she who lives on the side of Helicon,
the muse of luscious sight and lovely sorrow,
he who lives at Third and Houston,
the genius of murdered love—

Although he knows that without this last voyage
he would be only another ruined poet,
and this is his glory—Prince Street is his glory.
The truth is he has become his own sad poem,
he walks and eats and sleeps in total sadness,
sadness is even what he calls his life, he
is the teacher of sadness, there are no limits
to his bitter song, he sits at the long bar
across the street from New York Kitchen

drinking sadness—mixed with wine—
and it is his own regret that moves him to tears
and his own sorrow that saves him—he is saved
by his own sorrow—it is his victory—

And it is his victory that though he lay
bored and oppressed for the last ten years
he sang like no one else before him did
about himself and his own suffering.
He was the first, and since he wrote
in innocence both the remorse and pity
are almost forgivable. It is hard to think
of Coleridge without an Ovid first or Pound
alive in the cage without him. I myself
feel almost happy that he came before me,
that my own wailing
found such a model in his books of sorrow.
In my lighter moments when my cheeks
are dry and my heart is not yet pounding
I like to compare his heaviness to mine—
or mine to his—to see whose chair is older,
whose rug is thinner, whose hands are colder,
although the world I live and wander in
is really not like his, at least not yet—

And when the color south of Cooper Union
settles into mauve or streaky violet
I leave him lecturing his loyal wife
or cursing his rotten enemies
and make my way to the broken-down subway stop
at Spring and Broadway, humming in both languages,
the white moon above me, the dirt somewhere beneath me,
the sidewalks crazy again, the lights in Jersey,
the lights in Manhattan, like the fires in Rome,
burning again without me, I on the edge
of Empire walking west in the snow, my neck
now raw, my feet now raw, my eyes gone blind,
the last one on the streets, the last poet left
who lives like this, the last one who does a dance
because of the dirty ice and the leather boots,

alone in the middle of nowhere, no one to see
his gorgeous retrieval, no one to shake the air
with loud applause and no one to turn and bow to
in the middle of his exile ten cold minutes
before he leaves the street for his soft pillow
and his other exile, far from Rome's domain,
and far from New York's domain, now silent and peaceful.

# LEAVING ANOTHER KINGDOM

*For Phil Levine*

I think this year I'll wait for the white lilacs
before I get too sad.
I'll let the daffodils go, flower by flower,
and the blue squill, and the primroses.
Levine will be here by then,
waving fountain pens, carrying rolled-up posters
of Ike Williams and King Levinsky.
He will be reaching into his breast pocket
for maps of grim Toledo
showing the downtown grilles and the bus stations.
He and I together
will get on our hands and knees
on the warm ground
in the muddy roses
under the thorn tree.
We will walk the mile to my graveyard
without one word of regret,
two rich poets
going over the past a little,
changing a thing or two,
making a few connections,
doing it all with balance,
stopping along the way to pet a wolf,
slowing down at the locks,
giving each other lectures on early technology,
mentioning eels and snakes,
touching a little on our two cities,
cursing our Henrys a little,
his Ford, my Frick,
being almost human about it, almost decent,
sliding over the stones to reach the island,
throwing spears on the way,
staring for twenty minutes at two robins
starting a life together in rural Pennsylvania,
kicking a heavy tire, square and monstrous,
huge and soggy, maybe a '49 Hudson,
maybe a '40 Packard, maybe a Buick
with mohair seats and silken cords
and tiny panes of glass—both of us seeing
the same car, each of us driving

our own brick road, both of us whistling
the same idiotic songs, the tops of trees flying,
houses sailing along, the way they did then,
both of us walking down to the end of the island
so we could put our feet in the water, so I could
show him where the current starts, so we could
look for bottles and worn-out rubbers, Trojans
full of holes, the guarantee run out—
love gone slack and love gone flat—
a few feet away from New Jersey near the stones
that look like large white turtles guarding the entrance
to the dangerous channel where those lovers—Tristan
and his Isolt, Troilus and you know who,
came roaring by on inner tubes, their faces
wet with happiness, the shrieks and sighs
left up the river somewhere, now their fingers
trailing through the wake, now their arms out
to keep themselves from falling, now in the slow part
past the turtles and into the bend, we sitting there
putting on our shoes, he with Nikes,
me with Georgia loggers, standing up
and smelling the river, walking single file
until we reach the pebbles, singing in French
all the way back, losing the robins forever,
losing the Buick, walking into the water,
leaving another island, leaving another
retreat, leaving another kingdom.

# NEAR PÉRIGORD

On the first day of viburnum
I followed a school bus for five miles
past the magnolias and the copper lions
to the shad-men rocking and sleeping in their bleached boats.
I had just read Pound again and I was thinking
of his brain floating by me in the universe
and his dead body lying face up at Rapallo.
I picked him some violets, for his bitter nose,
and one or two strands of dry forsythia
for his empty hands, something to wave and wave
as he did his bitter business with Kung and Jefferson.
Later that day as I was driving past
my silver cliffs I stopped to pick him some grass,
and thought, if he could wait, I'd get him radishes
or daisies, when they come. Dead poets like him
are all for flowers, they still like to sniff
and stare in the air—vaguely—like sensitive horses,
their eyes filled up with grief and yearning.
If I had the casket before me I would put
a sunflower in the paw—he wouldn't mind—
as if he were lying there waiting to jump up,
waiting to shout, "it's me, it's me, I live
for beauty, I live for justice," and then sink back
on the satin pillow, his hair falling over the edges,
the crimson gone from his face, the yellow back.
—Dear poets of Périgord, dear poets of New York,
I stopped at a small park on the way back
to think about the centaurs and the white oxen.
I thought we'd share the light between us, I thought
we'd talk about Flaubert and his contempt
for *la bêtise moderne,* or for that matter
we could talk about the Venice of dreams
or we could turn to American poetry
since World War II and the function of government
to dirty the water or we could just sit and rage
at the new mushiness and the new anemia.
For silence he could stand there staring at the trees
or look at me in the face without a word,
the way he did at the end—for my own silence
I could go back to his death in '72

and what has happened to me in the last ten years
or I'd go back to 1948
and what it was like to read *Personae*, to sit
on the stone benches and read, or I'd return,
as I always do, to the hatred of Jews, to Pound's
own home-grown vicious boring *bêtise*, but mostly
I think my mind would drift away and the humming
and the breathing would just take over, a concentration
on something bright and tender, some dear memory
of southern France, the road below Carcassonne,
the smell of dust and rain. My last flower
was sticking out of the ash tray,
a piece of honeysuckle or mock orange,
and I was driving *up* the river. I ended
snorting the honeysuckle—that's what it was—
and watching the seals go by. I was thinking
of Wyndham Lewis, I think, when Pound disappeared,
and when he sang his bitter song again,
a kind of whistling on the passenger's side,
I was already looking at the orange sky
and thinking of the frog's glass throat and the green light
that gives him his wisdom, and I was thinking again—
one last time—of the steps of San Salvatore
and the towers floating in the water—1982,
City of Easton, the iron railroad bridges,
the old stone houses, the first American flag,
Age of the Reagans, horrible and disastrous.

# FOR SONG

I am sitting thirty feet above the water
with my hand at my throat,
listening to the owls go through the maples
and the seaplanes go up and down like cracked buzzsaws.

I am finding my own place
in the scheme of things
between the nation of Reuben half drunk on twisted coneflowers
and the nation of Dan all crazy for weird veronica.

I am paying attention to providence,
the silver hordes this time,
the mud up to my knees,
the glass on my fingers.

I am studying paradise and the hereafter,
a life beyond compare,
a great log thrown up for my own pleasure,
an unbelievably large and cold and beneficent sun.

I am lifting a blade of grass to my wet lips
for music;
I am trying a dozen fruits and flowers
to get one sound;

I am twisting my head around, I am slowly clapping
for harmony;
I am raising my eyes, I am listening to the worms
for song.

# MY SWALLOWS

For hours I sit here facing the white wall
and the dirty swallows. If I move too much,
I will lose everything, if I even breathe,
I'll lose the round chest and the forked tail
and the nest above the window, under the ceiling.

As far as shame, I think I have lived too long
with only the moonlight coming in to worry
too much about what it looks like. I have given
a part of my mind away, for what it's worth
I have traded half of what I have—

I'll call it half—so I can see these smudges
in the right light. I think I live in ruins
like no one else, I see myself as endlessly
staring at what I lost, I see me mourning
for hours, either worn away with grief

or touched with simple regret, but free this time
to give myself up to loss alone. I mourn
for the clumsy nest and I mourn for the two small birds
sitting up there above the curtains watching—
as long as I am there—and I mourn for the sky

that makes it clear and I mourn for my two eyes
that drag me over, that make me sit there singing,
or mumbling or murmuring, at the cost
of almost everything else, my two green eyes,
my brown—my hazel, flecked with green and brown—

and this is what I'll do for twenty more years,
if I am lucky—even if I'm not—I'll live
with the swallows and dip through the white shadows
and rest on the eaves and sail above the window.
This is the way I *have* lived, making a life

for more than twenty years—for more than forty—
out of this darkness; it was almost a joy,
almost a pleasure, not to be foolish or maudlin,
sitting against my wall, closing my eyes,
singing my dirges.

# BERKELEY

Today I saw the weird leg of Apollo
go in after Daphne—it was either cyprus
or Monterey pine, I am so blind and ignorant
of West Coast flora. I saw the wood waver
and the ground shake; I sat on my black briefcase
looking up at the leaves. I who am so
wondrous, I who always looked for Messiahs,
I who gave opinions, caught up now
in a new strangeness thousands of miles away
from my own cold river, learning quickly to eat
the other foods, learning to love
the way they do, walking after them
with my mouth half open, starting gently to teach,
doing the wind first, doing the dark old days
before there was even wind, saving Picasso
for Monday or Tuesday, saving the two dark strings
for Wednesday night, the night of the dozen tears,
saving New York
for the trip back to the airport, pushing the door
with tapered fingers, racing down the belt
with all that fire around me, sitting by the window
with only three minutes to go. Swinging my briefcase
with all the secrets inside. Keeping my secrets.
Thinking of Poland again. Getting ready for snow.

# THE DANCING

In all these rotten shops, in all this broken furniture
and wrinkled ties and baseball trophies and coffee pots
I have never seen a post-war Philco
with the automatic eye
nor heard Ravel's "Bolero" the way I did
in 1945 in that tiny living room
on Beechwood Boulevard, nor danced as I did
then, my knives all flashing, my hair all streaming,
my mother red with laughter, my father cupping
his left hand under his armpit, doing the dance
of old Ukraine, the sound of his skin half drum,
half fart, the world at last a meadow,
the three of us whirling and singing, the three of us
screaming and falling, as if we were dying,
as if we could never stop—in 1945—
in Pittsburgh, beautiful filthy Pittsburgh, home
of the evil Mellons, 5,000 miles away
from the other dancing—in Poland and Germany—
oh God of mercy, oh wild God.

# MOSCOW

*For Diane Freund*

I love to bend down over my love,
my crayon at her breast, my lips just over her neck.
I love her eyes following my left hand,
her fingers rubbing the Greek blanket.
I love the sunlight on the cold windows,
the horns of Scriabin rising through the dreary street,
the carved houses forever on our wild faces.

Look at our poor rhododendron
blooming its heart out
and our red petunias
trying to come to life in the wet dirt.

Look at the thorn tree
gone wild with seed
and the white lilacs
turning brown and spongy.

Look at my eyes
in the clear glass
and my hairy hand
coming to rest on the greasy sash.

Look at my heart there
underneath the white sweater.
Look at my two red lips
opening and closing again, look at them singing and dancing.

# BEE BALM

Today I'm sticking a shovel in the ground
and digging up the little green patch
between the hosta and the fringe bleeding heart.
I am going to plant bee balm there
and a few little pansies till the roots take
and the leaves spread out in both directions.

This is so the hummingbird will rage
outside my fireplace window; this is so
I can watch him standing in the sun
and hold him a little above my straining back,
so I can reach my own face up to his
and let him drink the sugar from my lips.

This is so I can lie down on the couch
beside the sea horse and the glass elephant,
so I can touch the cold wall above me
and let the yellow light go through me,
so I can last the rest of the summer on thought,
so I can live by secrecy and sorrow.

# VIVALDI YEARS

I lay forever, didn't I, behind those old windows,
listening to Bach and resurrecting my life.
I slept sometimes for thirty or forty minutes
while the violins shrieked and the cellos trembled.
It was a crazy youth, wasn't it, letting
my mind soar like that, giving myself
up to poetry the way I did.
It was a little like Goethe's, wasn't it,
a little like Eugene O'Neill's, one joyous
sadness after another. That was the everlasting
life, wasn't it. The true world without end.

# DUBUQUE STREET

If this were my lawn I would stand here staring
at the gray clouds moving across the small moon.

I would watch the flutter on the furthermost leaf
behind the rainspout and the crumbling brick.

I would plan the next twenty years without flinching,
one knee in the tomatoes,

one knee on the cement,
my hands all black from dreaming and digging and praying
in the soft dirt.

# HUZZA!

I know this life is a madness. I am lying
in another bed, listening to the words
of *Carmina Burana*, holding a pillow up
the way I do. I think I lie for hours
listening to music. I am becoming a sucker
for every sonata, every étude, every
Chinese baby sitting behind his bamboo
dreaming about his sticks and wires. I sometimes
leap to my feet when the piece is over, shouting
until the window rattles. I almost forget
my dead heart lying there, my rotten pajamas
and ugly robe, my floor with painted splinters,
the sound of violins in the empty room
sends such a shiver through my frozen body,
the sound of cellos by the mirror, an oboe
beside the fallen bed, The Primrose Concerto,
The Kreutzer—that young Chinese with the drooping wire,
that Li-Young Li. Ah Bravo! *Evivva!* Bravo!

# SAYING THE FIRST WORDS

I could live like that,
putting my chair by the window,
making my tea,
letting the light in,
trapping the spider in my left hand.

I could pull the one book down
and find my place inside the four worlds
and face the wrong way
and live forever by mercy and wisdom.

I could love the pine tree,
and the road going back and forth like a blue thread,
and the fire inside the hills,
and the grass going down to the river—my wildest dream.

# NIGHT AGAIN

I'm finally listening to my own radio
after a long and almost heartless day.

I'm folding my wings in front of my chest
and rubbing my beak through the inner feathers.

I'm warbling and warbling,
like some tenor from the 1940's,

matching song for song,
hating the sorrow with all my heart,

loving the pleasures, loving the sullen pockets,
reaching notes beyond my hearing or caring.

# TODAY A LEAF

*For William Merwin*

Today it was just a dry leaf that told me
I should live for love.
It wasn't the six birds sitting like little angels
in the white birch tree,
or the knife I use to carve my pear with.
It was a leaf, that had read Tolstoi, and Krishnamurti,
that had loved William James,
and put sweet Jesus under him where he could be safe forever.
"The world is so bright," he said. "You should see the light."
"We are born without defenses, both babies and leaves."
"The branch is necessary, but it is in the way."
"I am not afraid. I am never afraid."
Then he stretched his imaginary body
this way and that.
He weighs a half a gram, is brown and green,
with two large mold spots on one side, and a stem
that curls away, as if with a little pride,
and he could be easily swept up and forgotten,
but oh he taught me love for two good hours,
and helped me with starvation, and dread, and dancing.
As far as I'm concerned his grave is here
beside me,
next to the telephone and the cupful of yellow pencils,
under the window, in the rich and lovely presence
of Franz Joseph Haydn and Domenico Scarlatti and Gustav Mahler
forever.

# THE VOICE

Somewhere inside the Rio Hotel in a hall
that turns to the left, in a florid sumptuous hall
that turns and twists before it comes to rest,
I hear the voice of Edith Piaf remembering
the grief of this poor life; somewhere in a bed,
behind a piece of steel, I hear her moaning,
I hear it for the thousandth time, the mixture
of absolute sadness and absolute cunning, the voice
that lived on sound alone, that lived on anguish.

Somewhere across the street I wait on the wet
stone outside the Maccabeem, in the one
dry doorway. Somewhere I eat a half a sandwich
or sit at the table beside a weary Chasid,
tasting a little meat, a little soup,
and wait.

# THE NEW MOSES

Look at those poor cattails
putting up with the noise of engines.
Look at them using that great wind
in their own lives.
They will be all that's left
when the airport is dismantled
and the city is gone
and the roads are ruined and scattered.
Some new Moses will float by then
and some sad princess will find him
and kiss him a thousand times on his eyes and nose
before she gives him up.
She will stand one minute in the throne room,
or in the hallway staring through the glass,
and almost run, and almost fall,
as she makes her way down through the buried brick and iron
on the almost forgotten fringes of modern Thebes,
not far from the man-made islands and lost skyways,
the hundred heavily guarded tunnels and bridges,
of ancient New York.

# SINGING

I have been waiting for a month
for this squirrel to dissolve in water.
I couldn't afford the disgrace
of dumping it on to the ground
and watching its body lurch and its teeth chatter.

There is such ghoulishness now
that it might drag its back legs after it,
such desperation
that I might rub its shoulders or brush its lips
to bring it back to life.

You who rushed home to masturbate,
you who touched the same red flower every day,
you know how I must skirt this lawn
to avoid the barrel.
You know how I live in silence.

You who knelt on the frozen leaves,
you know how dark it got under the ice;
you know how hard it was to live
with hatred, how long it took to convert
death and sadness into beautiful singing.

# THE SEINE AT NIGHT

You would have to see Virgil Thomson creeping down here,
studying most of all these oily shadows
and see his face in the water
with a doorway behind it
to know that those horns are just the ticket,
and those edgy violins,
and that long slow resonant snare.

The applause too,
the water lapping up the stone steps,
a piece of light wood against the window,
a barrel rolling down the floor;
paper on fire,
cracking and spluttering for five minutes
before it goes out.

This loverboy from K.C.,
this judge,
this collaborator.
Virgil the Baptist,
the perfect transplant,
the half-mother of us all,
our Vivaldi.

# AT JANE'S

*For Gil Orlovitz, 1919–1974*

I touch the rose to see what happens there
before I go inside to eat, I pull
the clothesline down and kick the cracked cement,
I howl to myself for mercy. One more time
I walk through the rotten tomatoes. I will end
with little leaves on my shoes, with spoonfuls of mud,
with a beating heart, with a mouth that's open—
I hold my arm out straight like a dirty drunk,
I walk the plank between the rhododendron
and the little pear. For all I know
I could live here happy, I could walk
from here to the river and back without a thought.
I could stop at the Super-America
and read the morning paper. I could sit
at my pancake dreaming of heaven, smiling like a lamb,
listening vaguely to all the garbage, finding
my cave and my twine, my dark place, chewing and listening
while inside I wander—I beg for justice—I crawl
through hell for a little justice. I turn to the wall
and sing a little, and dance a little—
just as the fall is breaking on the Ohio,
the leaves are turning yellow, in Marietta,
the backyards stretching out for hundreds of yards
the way they do in America, all that richness,
all that Utopia, wasted, a little dog
howling out there, inside we're barking, inside
I'm finding another heaven, I'm turning around
this way and that, I'm finding my hole in the sun . . .
We're talking now about Spanish music, the difference
in soul between northern Europe and southern Europe;
we're talking now about Crete, we're talking
about Robert Lowell and Delmore Schwartz; I'm lecturing
on Orlovitz, I'm talking about his sonnets,
I'm talking about his death on West End Avenue,
about the poet we lost, about his life,
about the dull politics of poesy,
about the nineteenth century, about Keats,
eighty miles from Wheeling, West Virginia,
a million miles from Rome. Poor Orlovitz,
he wrote 500 poems. I remember the letters:

"Is this a poem, could you send me twenty bucks?"
What do I do with him now? He fell in the street
in front of a doorman; oh his death was superb,
the doorman blew his whistle, Orlovitz climbed
into a yellow cab, he'd never disappoint
a doorman. Now I'm brooding a little, absent,
the way I get, listening to the refrigerator,
the only music we have in North America,
cursing the Reagans a little, saying inside
one of Orlovitz's poems, going back again
into the cave, remembering Shelley's words
about his cave, and Vergil's, and Milton's, knowing
that mine is like theirs, a half mile underground,
where you go on your knees, where you keep the candle outside—
the underground journey—shivers and tremblings. We walk
to the river after breakfast, I'm in heaven,
I saw the meadow, I heard the voices, I felt
the light on my face—in Marietta, Ohio—
with Rachael Stern and Jack Killian and Jane
Somerville, there are alleys between the yards,
it is the oldest city in Ohio,
I wore my black suit for the reading, I roared
and whispered through forty poems, I sat like a lamb
in the mayor's living room, I sat like a dove
eating cheese and smiling, talking and smiling,
thinking my thoughts, my wise and tender thoughts,
the mayor's palace, Marietta, Ohio.

# JOHN'S MYSTERIES

I've been seeing these tombstone beef sticks
and that umbrella tree in so many cities
that I forget where it is I am,
whether it's dirty John's I'm standing in line in
with onions and T-bone steaks in my hands,
or Bishop's, I think it was Bishop's, with hard salami,
safflower mayonnaise and two-percent milk.
My own system of perfect retrieval
tells me it's a big-leaved catalpa,
not an umbrella tree, and what it grows
is not cigars, but intricate seed stalks, terrible
to smoke, cancerless, tasteless, drooping and beautiful.
But I believe only in the islands
so I will insist on emptying the parking lot
of the two beer trucks and putting a table there
under the cigar tree, for me and my friends to eat at.
We will take three hours and end by turning
on the lights and leaning back in exhaustion.
We will be so happy about where we are
that we will cry for sadness, cursing everything
and anything from changed emotional conditions
to polluted leaves to emigration laws
that could threaten to end our mysteries and pleasures.
We will keep the napkins as souvenirs
and write, in ink, what it was like to live here
on Gilbert Street and Market, on Sixth and Pine,
in a town in Crete eight miles from Omalos,
a mile or so from the crone and her great-granddaughter
selling warm Coca-Colas on the flat
at the end of the deepest gorge in Europe—
if Crete is in Europe—at a lovely table with lights
hanging from the trees, a German there to remind us
of the Parachute Corps in 1941,
a Turk for horror, a Swede for humor, an Israeli
to lecture us, the rest of us from New Jersey
and California and Michigan and Georgia,
eating the lamb and drinking the wine, adoring it,
as if we were still living on that sea,
as if in Crete there had not been a blossom,
as if it had not fallen in Greece and Italy,

some terrible puzzle in great Knossos
Sir Arthur Evans is still unravelling,
the horrors spread out in little pieces
as if it were a lawn sale or foreclosure.
—I like to think of it that way, him on the grass there
putting together our future, the seven of us,
the eight of us, by the sea—looking at Libya—
this way, looking that way, this way, that way,
watching him with curiosity and terror,
wondering if he'll get it right, wondering how much
it's really in his hands, wanting a little
to tamper with it, getting a little irritated
with so much of it lying on the ground,
wanting it to be as it once was,
wanting the bull to bellow,
wanting him to snort and shake the ground,
wanting it to be luminous again,
Daedalus and Minos, Pasiphaë squealing with love,
the dear Parisian with her breasts exposed,
little courtyards where we could see the light,
little airways and passageways, pretty steps
going up and down, those parapets where friends
could look at the waves and talk about their sorrows,
those giant jars where all our wines and oils
were stored, those paintings that made us remember, those flutes
that made us dance, that put a lilt in our walk—
Our lives are in his hands, he goes through his wallet
to see if he has money to pay the bearers;
he touches his chest to see if he will die
before his work is done, he puts his camera
in front of the sun, he finds another fragment
that tells him something, he is cradling his elbow,
he is touching his chin, to help him think—
Sir Arthur Evans, angel of death—I walk
up Gilbert Street to reach my house. I live
with music now, and dance, I lie alone
waiting for sweetness and light. I'm balanced forever
between two worlds, I love what we had, I love
dreaming like this, I'm finding myself in the charts
between the white goat and the black, between

the trade with Sicily and the second palace, between
the wave of the sea and the wave of the sky, I am
a drop of white paint, I am the prow of a ship,
I am the timbers, I am the earthquake—
in eighty or ninety years
someone will dream of Crete again and see me
sitting under this tree and study me
along with the baskets and the red vases.
I'll walk across here touching one beer truck
with my left hand and one with my other.
I'll put my old stone arms around his neck
and kiss him on the lip and cheek, I'll sing
again and again
until he remembers me, until he remembers
the green catalpa pushing through the cement
and the little sticks of meat inside, his own
wild voyage behind him, his own sad life ahead.

# SOAP

Here is a green Jew
with thin black lips.
I stole him from the men's room
of the Amelia Earhart and wrapped him in toilet paper.
Up the street in *Parfumes*
are Austrian Jews and Hungarian,
without memories really,
holding their noses in the midst of that
paradise of theirs.
There is a woman outside
who hesitates because it is almost Christmas.
"I think I'll go in and buy a Jew," she says.
"I mean some soap, some nice new lilac or lily
to soothe me over the hard parts,
some Zest, some Fleur de Loo, some Wild Gardenia."

And here is a blue Jew.
It is his color, you know,
and he feels better buried in it, imprisoned
in all that sky, the land of death and plenty.
If he is an old one he dances,
or he sits stiffly,
listening to the meek words and admiring the vile actions
of first the Goths and then the Ostrogoths.
Inside is a lovely young girl,
a Dane, who gave good comfort
and sad support to soap of all kinds and sorts
during the war and during the occupation.
She touches my hand with unguents and salves.
She puts one under my nose all wrapped in tissue,
and squeezes his cheeks.

I buy a black Rumanian for my shelf.
I use him for hair and beard,
and even for teeth when things get bitter and sad.
He had one dream, this piece of soap,
if I'm getting it right,
he wanted to live in Wien
and sit behind a hedge on Sunday afternoon
listening to music and eating a tender schnitzel.

That was delirium. Other than that he'd dream
of America sometimes, but he was a kind of cynic,
and kind of lazy—conservative—even in his dream,
and for this he would pay, he paid for his lack of dream.
The Germans killed him because he didn't dream
enough, because he had no vision.

I buy a brush for my back, a simple plastic
handle with gentle bristles. I buy some dust
to sweeten my body. I buy a yellow cream
for my hairy face. From time to time I meet
a piece of soap on Broadway, a sliver really,
without much on him, sometimes I meet two friends
stuck together the way those slivers get
and bow a little, I bow to hide my horror,
my grief, sometimes the soap is so thin
the light goes through it, these are the thin old men
and thin old women the light goes through, these are
the Jews who were born in 1865
or 1870, for them I cringe, for them
I whimper a little, they are the ones who remember
the eighteenth century, they are the ones who listened
to heavenly voices, they were lied to and cheated.

My counterpart was born in 1925
in a city in Poland—I don't like to see him born
in a little village fifty miles from Kiev
and have to fight so wildly just for access
to books, I don't want to see him struggle
half his life to see a painting or just to
sit in one of the plush chairs listening to music.
He was dragged away in 1940
and turned to some use in 1941,
although he may have fought a little, piled
some bricks up or poured some dirty gasoline
over a German truck. His color was rose
and he floated for me for days and days; I love
the way he smelled the air, I love how he looked,
how his eyes lighted up, how his cheeks were almost pink
when he was happy. I loved how he dreamed, how he almost
disappeared when he was in thought. For him

I write this poem, for my little brother, if I
should call him that—maybe he is the ghost
that lives in the place I have forgotten, that dear one
that died instead of me—oh ghost, forgive me!—
Maybe he stayed so I could leave, the *older* one
who stayed so I could leave—oh live forever!
forever!—Maybe he is a Being from the other
world, his left arm agate, his left eye crystal,
and he has come back again for the twentieth time,
this time to Poland, to Warsaw or Bialystok,
to see what hell is like. I think it's that,
he has come back to live in our hell, if he could
even prick his agate arm or even weep
with those crystal eyes—oh weep with your crystal eyes,
dear helpless Being, dear helpless Being. I'm writing this
in Iowa and Pennsylvania and New York City,
in time for Christmas, 1982,
the odor of Irish Spring, the stench of Ivory.

# I PITY THE WIND

I am taking off my glasses
so I can stare at the little candles
and the glass of water
in pure darkness.

I am letting a broom stand
for my speech on justice
and an old thin handkerchief
for the veil of melodrama I have worn for thirty years.

I am dragging in Euripides
for his strange prayer
and my own true Hosea
for his poem on love and loyalty.

After a minute I fall down dead
from too much thought
and turn to the freezing wall
for an hour of quiet sadness.

I start my practice later,
twenty minutes for breathing,
twenty minutes for song,
twenty minutes for liberation and ritual.

My poem is about the airshaft
and Zoroaster
and the soul caught in its last struggle
with the two-headed cow, father of everything.

My elation has something to do with light,
my misery with darkness,
my secrecy and fear and distance
with neither.

I end up with a pillow
and a painted floor, as I always do,
my head on the flowers, a little pocket for air,
my right arm drifting and dangling.
.   .   .

I end up just humming,
true to myself at last,
preparing myself for the bridge
and the hand that will lead me over, the hand I adore.

I pity this hero,
so in love with fire,
so warlike,
so bent on teaching.

Before the winter is over I'll have some sticks
for my dining room table and one or two large blooms
to take the place of the Norfolk pine
shredding and popping in the cold rain.

I'll pick some berries from the thin viburnum
and eat them as a bird does, one at a time,
jerking my head and looking around with terror,
studying the world with softened eyes.

I'll walk between the kitchen and the birch tree
a hundred times, a broom in one hand and either
a shovel or an ax in the other. I'll tie
a piece of frozen string around my finger

and either chew some bark or do a little
Esquimaux shuffling, and moaning, around the broken
circle of slate. I'll look for either a robin
or some other monster, maybe a yellow warbler

to go with my scarf. I'll count the days till Easter,
the thirteen Sundays, the Virgin Days, the Martyr Days,
the days of sleep and waking. Groundhog Day.
Valentine's Day. Ninety days in all.

The one or two cars that come by will be farting
their brains out trying to make it in the cold,
and no one will see me dying there in the twilight,
holding my hands up in the slippery branches.

I'll stay for ten more minutes before I go in,
enjoying the cold and letting the ice come into
my lungs and heart. Whatever my struggle is
I'll let it take place in this yard where the pile of stones

was, and the little hill—I'll keep it
between one tree and another, mostly away
from the flower bed and the wall, as close as I can
to the cement steps and the walk. I'll say goodnight

. . .

to one thing or another, maybe a headlight
from Route 6ll, maybe a brilliant oriole
come here to die in the dark. I'll drink my tea
and my Popov over the heater and with a knife

and screwdriver I'll scrape the snow from my boots.
I'll rest for six good hours and start my watch
again at six in the morning—who's to say
what happens in the night?—I'll look for a jay

to start me right, some pale-crested bluejay
lost and gone wild, some giant from the south
remembering his pine, some frightened animal
screaming for life, sliding on the branches,

wanting his meadow back. I'll pick him up,
though it's too late to put him inside my coat
against my chest, and it's too late to breathe
into his bony mouth. I'll wait for three

minutes, to do him justice, then I'll start
my icy walk—a part of the mystery—
and end up shaking my feathers from the cold,
a monster myself, with a piece of the loblolly

in my hip pocket, deciding, certainly before
Washington's Birthday, and certainly before Mother's Day,
whether it was worth it for our birds
to come so far for their wisdom, little simulacra

dying, as I do, from hunger and disease,
maybe two more to go today, the bastard
love and the bastard hope, maybe three,
the bastard pity, before I pull the blind up

and look at the moon, full and weeping tonight,
although it's past its prime and getting ready
for the last sliver again, then darkness again
and the first sliver again, ferocious phases.

# ROMANCE

After thirty years
I am still listening to the pipes,
I am still enchanted
with the singing and moaning of the dry boards.

I am lying there night after night
thinking of water.
I am joining palms, or whistling Mozart
and early Yeats.

I am living without savagery,
stretching my body and turning on my left side
for music,
humming to myself and turning on my right side
for words.

# VILLA-LOBOS

I don't know if it's the one great sadness of my life
that I have to return this way every night
to the same small yard and the same small tree
and touch the buds and pick the ancient leaves
or if it's the one great joy. Let there be
one blue space in the sky above to match
the blue between the branches. Let there be
spaces between the chords to match
the spaces between the leaves. It took me
half a life to come here, one small house
on a battered hill, one small tree
to match the house, a man against the tree
with cello strings in his hand, a little dull gleaming
to match his gleaming, a little sobbing
to match his own, a kind of painful sliding
from string to string to match the hill
or the house itself, or even the man himself,
his elbow out in space, his left eye shut,
his heart already bursting from the tender sounds.

# THE NETTLE TREE

Mine was the nettle tree, the nettle tree.
It grew beside the garage and on the river
and I protected it from all destroyers.

I loved the hanging branches and the trunk
that grew like a pole. I loved the little crown
that waved like a feather. I sat for hours watching

the birds come in to eat the berries. I read
my Homer there—I wanted to stay forever
sleeping and dreaming. I put my head on the trunk

to hear my sounds. It was my connection for years,
half hanging in the wind—half leaning, half standing.
It was my only link. It was my luxury.

# SYCAMORE

It was March third I came outside and saw
for the first time the buttonwood tree with last year's
leaves hanging in the wind like little hearts
and one or two crazy birds going mad with choices
in the hideous leftover snow and the slippery mud.
March the third. The branches were more a silver
than either green or tan, there was no fuzz
yet. Spring was still in Arizona, the Sonora
desert somewhere, somewhere in Ensenada,
and we were still gluing our frozen ears
to our crystal sets in Fairchild and Waterloo.
    The lower branches bend as if they were holding
castanets in their hands—this tree is Greek!—
maybe as if they were limp, the left hand is limp,
it is a tree from Greenwich Avenue,
from Fire Island, but the upper arms
reach out to plead for mercy, reach out to bless
us, she is a twenty-arm goddess, leaning
over a little, dancing her dance, making
little obscene gestures to the lord of lords,
a tiny finger here, a whole fist there.
    I open the windows, I pull the wooden strips
away from the sashes, I tear the dirty plastic,
I let the sun in. Soon my ties will be dancing,
soon my poems will be on the floor, I am
old Shivers, I do a turn to the left, to the right.
Where shall I go this year? What door will I open
and put a little primitive iron against?
Where shall I put the bucket? I want to live here
beside my tree and watch it change, the brown
give way to green, the green give way to brown.
I want, for once, to understand what happens
when the skin falls off. This tree is like a snake.
How many years does it live? What does it do
in its sleep? March thirty-first, this year,
is the little passage; we will get on our knees
and howl with freedom, not one of us can bear
to live without howling, we were given voices
so we could scream. I sing a song from Florida
about the life to come, someone is singing—

she is a flute, I am a silver harp—
about the seven openings, the soul
skittering, sacred things. I want her to go
so I can become a tree, so I can bury
myself as Daphne does, she is the one
who understands what it means to be tormented;
she calls the spring Apollo, Apollo tortured her,
he followed her from one bare tree to another.
I call it Apollo too, I take my place
inside the silver wood, at least for a year.
Next March the third I'll struggle out of my skin
like a sleepy girl, my hair will be too dry,
my nails too long, my mouth will start to work,
at first it will be too hoarse, and then too shrill;
I'll see the streets will be empty, there will be peace,
I'll walk to the graveyard and back, I'll walk to the lake,
no one will see me, no one will follow me
with rage in his eyes, with brutal love in his hands.
It is like death, isn't it, living in the tree,
listening to what were noises, feeling those changes
and knowing they weren't for you—I love the bells
when they come, I love standing in a grove
and guessing which one she's in—I'm in—if I were
Apollo I'd turn myself into this sycamore
and reach my arms through hers, I'd do some flashy
two-step that's made for heavy sycamores,
and when we lie it would be like two great animals,
sweat running down our faces, tears down our legs.
    This year when I sit at the table with bitter bread
in my hands I'll stop for one full minute to give
some lonely praise to the sycamore; I'll say,
let's stop a minute and think of the sycamore,
let's think of the lovely white branches, let's think of the bark,
let's think of the leaves, the three great maple lobes.
What does it know of liberation? I'll say.
What does it know of slavery, bending over
the streams of America? How does it serve as a text
for lives that are pinched, or terrified? Were there sycamores
along the banks of the Rhine or Oder? Tell me
about its bells again, those most of all,

the hard gray balls that dangle from the stems,
tell me about the bark, the large thin flakes,
and the colors, dark at the bottom, light at the top.
And I will go on for an hour storming and raving
before I drink my final cup of wine
and shout to the Egyptians—as I do every year—
you are my Apollo, you are my fleshpot, forgive me
for turning into a tree, forgive me, you lovers
of life for leaving you suddenly, how foolish
and cheated you must have felt, how foolish the body
must feel when it's only a carcass, when the breath
has left it forever, as it always does,
in search of something painless; and I'll end
by sprinkling the tree and sprinkling the ground around it
and holding my hand up for a second of silence,
since I am the one who runs the service—I am
the only one in this house, I do my reclining
all alone, I howl when I want, and I am,
should anyone come in, a crooked tree
leaning far out, I am a hundred feet tall,
I am a flowering figure, I am staggering
across the desert, and here I am now in New York
and here I am now in Pittsburgh, the perfect wilderness.

# BAJA

These tiny Mexican mosquitoes are like lost souls
looking for blood among the white visitors
in their own land. They come to lead us through
some four or five old trees. They stoop to bite
our hands, they make that wailing sound I live
in terror of, they sing in our ears, they walk
between the seams, they reach for the drink they love,
they bend half over drinking,
they walk along the sand and through the flowers,
they look for work, they are looking for work, they pound
on the windows of our casita shouting *trabajo*,
*trabajo*, casting mournful eyes on the sea-wrack,
touching the broken sewer line and pointing
at the broken steps.
                    I catch one in a bottle
of Hellmann's and I let it loose outside
on the little plaza where the Citation is parked.
I tell him, my blood is for you, I tell him, remember
one Pennsylvanian who stopped to talk with the souls
and listened to them even if there was murder
and hatred between us; I ask about my future
as if I were Odysseus in hell
and he were Tiresias, that dear old lady,
or some other dead one, a Hercules or an Ajax.
He tells me, I think, to look out for my own
soul in the years to come, he tells me how long
it will be before I can rest a little, although
what he calls rest it may be some other thing
he talks about. He tells me there is a tree
and a yellow rock and a cloud. I should go left
around the tree, I should walk over the rock,
I should walk under the cloud; it is a Mexican
vision, full of darkness and secrecy.
I thank him for his kindness. Maybe he said
there is a room with terrible noises, tie
yourself to the kitchen table, hold your left hand
over your mouth, concentrate on living
a week at a time, divide your life into threes,
the terror can be digested, take care of yourself
when you are in New York, when you are sleeping,

when you are dying, there is a life to come—
or maybe he said, I love you more than anything,
have pity on me, please help me, take me with you,
I want the chance to live again, I can't
believe how large your limes were, oh I can't
believe how huge and clean your markets were;
take me with you, take me with you, wailing
and howling in front of me, in back of me,
pulling me down, the way they do, a swarm
of spirits, stumbling, pushing; I had to run,
I had to slam the door, I stood there freezing,
blood on the walls where I killed them, blood on my palms,
my forehead foolishly pounding, my two hands shaking,
all alone in the darkness, a man of the heart
making plans to the end, a screen for the terror,
a dish for the blood, a little love for strangers,
a little kindness for insects, a little pity for the dead.

# OF BLESSED NAME

Here in this huge dining room
with its crimson and gold-flocked wallpaper
and its etched glass and nude paintings and brass trimmings
I think of Spinoza sitting at his own table,
practicing what he believed in,
the good days.

And over there in the fish tank
with the pipe of white oxygen
going in and out of the lobster's last redoubt
I think of the red salmon and the pink flounder
as a backdrop to his thought.

Water was his main element.
Only then could God be understood
in all his modes.
The salmon loved him for this;
the lobster in all his fury grudgingly acknowledged his genius.

He dragged God into everything.
It gave him his distance.
It made him dream and figure twenty-four hours a day.

It kept the world at bay,
the carp going over and under
the bamboo bridge,
the mussels in white gravel,
the living grasses.
It kept it wonderful and flowing.

No one was ever more pure
or logical.
Even the crab loved him,
the bow-legged crab,
eternal enemy of the lobster.

I think of him here in Florida
under the boring chandelier,
a thousand little glass tassels going this way and that,
a carpet to keep him warm,
a fish tank to amuse him;

and I save him for the shameful end,
his lungs half filled with glass,
his body weak with fever,
carefully sealing a letter,
wisely adding a word here and there,
saying something terrifying,
saying something perfect and sweet and exact
as always.

# KISSING STIEGLITZ GOODBYE

Every city in America is approached
through a work of art, usually a bridge
but sometimes a road that curves underneath
or drops down from the sky. Pittsburgh has a tunnel—

you don't know it—that takes you through the rivers
and under the burning hills. I went there to cry
in the woods or carry my heavy bicycle
through fire and flood. Some have little parks—

San Francisco has a park. Albuquerque
is beautiful from a distance; it is purple
at five in the evening. New York is Egyptian,
especially from the little rise on the hill

at 14-C; it has twelve entrances
like the body of Jesus, and Easton, where I lived,
has two small floating bridges in front of it
that brought me in and out. I said goodbye

to them both when I was 57. I'm reading
Joseph Wood Krutch again—the second time.
I love how he lived in the desert. I'm looking at the skull
of Georgia O'Keeffe. I'm kissing Stieglitz goodbye.

He was a city, Stieglitz was truly a city
in every sense of the word; he wore a library
across his chest; he had a church on his knees.
I'm kissing him goodbye; he was, for me,

the last true city; after him there were
only overpasses and shopping centers,
little enclaves here and there, a skyscraper
with nothing near it, maybe a meaningless turf

where whores couldn't even walk, where nobody sits,
where nobody either lies or runs; either that
or some pure desert: a lizard under a boojum,
a flower sucking the water out of a rock.
.   .   .

What is the life of sadness worth, the bookstores
lost, the drugstores buried, a man with a stick
turning the bricks up, numbering the shards,
dream twenty-one, dream twenty-two. I left

with a glass of tears, a little artistic vial.
I put it in my leather pockets next
to my flask of Scotch, my golden knife and my keys,
my joyful poems and my T-shirts. Stieglitz is there

beside his famous number; there is smoke
and fire above his head; some bowlegged painter
is whispering in his ear; some lady-in-waiting
is taking down his words. I'm kissing Stieglitz

goodbye, my arms are wrapped around him, his photos
are making me cry; we're walking down Fifth Avenue;
we're looking for a pencil; there is a girl
standing against the wall—I'm shaking now

when I think of her; there are two buildings, one
is in blackness, there is a dying poplar;
there is a light on the meadow; there is a man
on a sagging porch. I would have believed in everything.

# TWO TREES

This is where I reach for the scarlet bud
and this is where I snap the little chicken claw
twenty feet from the water. Daylight has come
to the Iowa River amidst the blaring of horns
and the frantic splashing across the bridge. I stand
on the northeast corner in the upper branches
of two interlocking maples. I am engaged
in a ritual silence. I am listening to leaves
and flowers come. I look into the river
for backward spills and eddies, I look into the hills
for dreams and losses. There are two silver maples
half buried in water, starting to bud; there is
the shadow of pigeons under me; there is
a path with stones and a golden willow. I live
for this silence now. I stay in the tree. I think
like a bird for five or ten minutes. I see the cloud
on the water, I see the food. There is a Japanese
tulip tree a minute away from the river
half sitting in a sea of petals, there is
a day, or two, left, the weather is cold, I walk
like a man, like a human being, through the curled flowers,
I almost can't stand the beauty, the insides are white,
the color is in the veins, they are like onions
when you tear them apart, there is an odor; my house
is eighty yards away, I go there to think
and write, I put the blossoms down, I live there
beside them for two or three days, I line them up
on my table, it is my void, a dancing table,
a plastic cover, with other blossoms, some of them
floating as if they were seeds, it is the only
void I know, the only emptiness.

# ONE BIRD TO LOVE FOREVER

If I were to pick one bird to love forever
it would be the desert sparrow, sweetest
thing to ever live in Arizona,
sweetest thing of Mexico. I'd hold it
against my neck where the blood goes through, that soft
little nest underneath the chin, and stare at its eye
to hold it still, to keep it quiet. I'd let it
flutter, or let it fly, if it wanted. I'd rest
beside the acacia, beside the ironwood; I'd sit
for hours listening and loving.
                          When it flies
it rises like a junco, quick and crazy
to get away, and when it sits the softness of
birds is in its throat and chest. It has two
stripes, that is how we know it, one on the eye
and one extending down from the corner of the mouth
to make a pattern, white against the black,
and it has secret habits, it builds its nest
in some demented brush a hundred miles
from water—it never drinks, it seems to live
on nothing—I call it nothing but naturally
it thrives there. Joseph Wood Krutch, when he writes about the desert,
reminds us always that it is a paradise
for whatever lives there, the crazy trees, the lizards,
and nothing is deprived there, and nothing suffers,
it is their world, the funny quails and doves,
the sun shines on the needles, the spiders are huge,
the ground is always dry.
                     It is a madness
to think of loving that bird again. How could I
go back there anyhow? How would I live?
What would I do, go out to touch the thorns
and smell the flowers? Stand beside the boojum
and stare at the sky? Smile again like a lizard?
And Krutch is right—he's mostly right—the loving
of birds is useless, there is no true connection
between their lives and ours, they are only ideas.
It's always been that way, except when I read him—
I read him over and over—I see him using
his own bitterness as I have always used mine

to hide his weak heart behind, although the heart,
he'd say, is something like the liver, only coarser,
and he'd prefer the kidneys again for the seat
of all that soft emotion.                    I only spent
five days in the desert but I'm going to drive
from Mexico to Salt Lake City next time.
My sparrow ranges from Texas to California
and north into Nevada and Idaho.
There is a photo in Cruikshank, she is perched
on the edge of her nest and four huge mouths are screaming
for food; the nest is almost buried between
the pads of a heavy cactus and the spines—
two inches, three inches long—surround the nest,
it looks like one or two go through the twisted
grass itself, but somehow they seem indifferent,
the delicate babies, the mother. I want to touch
the thorns and see how sharp the needles are.
I want to live there, I think, wake up with the sun
on my face, wake up with the light making a diamond
or hexagram on my chest and arms and glide
to the sink to drink my water, like a gecko.
My dream of dreams has me staring out the window,
my blue pants are held up by a rope,
and my elbows are leaning on a wooden washboard.
She looks at me for a second. She. A chittering
sparrow. Almost eating her way through the glass.
And then she moves to her tree, a hundred miles
away, for all I know, from my world, this silly
and rotten concrete shack, a poet's ugly
home away from home, a little flowerpot
holding the window up, a vague amazement
to her, a curiosity.                    I look at the wind,
if you can look at the wind, and then I walk
for twenty or thirty minutes so I can find
my kidney on the road; I want to see it
weeping with pure self-pity, wringing its hands
the way a kidney wrings its hands, much better
than the liver, much better than the heart, more sadness

than either other organ. If I stand still,
if you catch me just right there is a cactus growing
out of my shoulder and my glasses are falling
as always; there is a look of wretched wisdom
on my red face—maybe there'll be a feather
with little bits of white on the outer edge
I'll put in my left pocket, maybe the stone
that goes with the feather, a tiny bit of pearl
to hold it down, you must hold feathers down,
and tiny bits of sand for the other pocket,
something to give me the desert again when I want it,
the blazing sunlight for grief, a little shade for the sorrow.

# FRITZ

This is too good for words. I lie here naked
listening to Kreisler play. It is the touch
I love, that sweetness, that ease. I saw him once
at the end of the 40's, in Pittsburgh, I thought what he did
had something to do with his being old, his moving
to the front of the stage, his talking and smiling. I study
the cracks in the ceiling, the painted floors. I love him
because he strayed from the art, because he finished
his formal training at twelve, because he was whimsical
and full of secret humors. He is another one
I missed—I'm sick about it—there is no table
for us, no chairs to sit on, no words to remember.
He knew both Schönberg and Brahms, he visited
Dvořák, he studied theory with Bruckner,
he was a friend of Caruso's, he was a friend
of Pablo Casals.
                    Something like terror moves me,
walking on 611. What have we lost?
Does Kreisler belong to the dead? Was that a world
of rapture that he lived in? In what year
did he fix his imagination? Will there be strings
two hundred years from now? Will there be winds?
—There is a bank that leads down from the towpath
and I have walked there a thousand times, each time
half tripping over a certain root—I think
it is the root of a locust, maybe a lilac.
Tonight I am partly moody, partly in dread,
there is some pain in my neck, but I am still
possessed a little. I rush into the living room
to listen to either the Elgar or the Mendelssohn.
Something left us forever in 1912,
or 1914. Now we live off the rot.
I wonder if it's true. Kreisler was fifty
when he came back to Paris, over seventy
when I saw him in 1948. The root
was in the nineteenth century. I'm lost,
I'm lost without that century. There is
one movement left. *Con amore.* I began
*my* journey in 1947. I wrote
four hours a day, I read five books a week.

I had to read five books. I never knew
the right hand was raised like that. I never knew
how trapped the body was. I didn't believe
you gave yourself to the fire like that, that after
awhile—if the brain was in the fingers—the heart
was all that made the sound, whatever I mean
by "sound," and that we have to start with feeling—
we poor machines—which stood me in good stead
for ten or twenty years, that and Marlowe's
tears, and Coleridge's soft flight, and Dostoevski's
rack—it was the fire that moved me.

I always remember the crone. I always think of her
at that card table selling us Cokes. I sit in Dante's
drinking my coffee, my left hand is walking through Crete,
my right hand is lying exhausted on the roof
looking up at the stars. It was the stars
that helped me then. I stood on the cracked cement
on the same hill I know where Minos stood
looking for heavenly bulls and for the first time
in Greece I had my lightness. I saw the link
between that life and mine, I saw the one
outside me stand for my own, like Dante himself
in Paradise. I felt I was standing inside
the sky, that there were other lights below me
and other worlds and this one could be restored.
And there were other feelings I have forgotten
or can't quite put in words. I saw myself
moving from body to body. I saw my own
existence taken from me. I lost the center.
—It lasted for fifteen minutes, then I slept,
with three or four others, scattered on that roof
as if we each had little rooms, the brilliance
of the night keeping us quiet, all our efforts—
at least my own—going into lying still,
going into some secret humming and adoring,
I was so changed, I was so small and silent.

In Crete the heart gets filled up, there is a joy
there, it is the mountains and sea combined,
it is the knowledge you have that there was a life
there for centuries, half unknown to Europe, half
unknown to Asia, Crete is a kind of moon
to me, a kind of tiny planet,
going through the same revolutions, over and over.
That was the first time I had been in the stars
for maybe twenty years, and it was odd
that I was not in the woods or on the water
in upper Michigan or Maine or Canada,
thousands of miles from civilization, now
it was thousands of years, although it was almost the same.
I dreamed of my bus ride back, some perfect village

in the mountains, and I dreamed of staring through the window
at some small child in blue or smiling at a man
with huge boots on. I wanted to sit in the square,
what little square there was, and talk again
about the ancient cities and the forest
that once filled Crete before I returned again
to my little room on the roof and my crazy pillow
and my sky of bitter lovers and animals,
three hundred miles from Africa, from Egypt.

It wasn't lost on me that it was Dante's
Café that I was sitting in—a coffee house
in Greenwich Village with an overblown photo
of Florence on the wall, squeezed in among
my loved ones, reading books, or talking, or waiting
for someone to come, for someone new to walk in
and catch our interest, the irony—even the comedy—
wasn't lost on me. I think I had been there
over an hour frowning and writing. It was
a disgrace! Thank God for New York! Thank God for tolerance!
Thank God for envy! Except that in New York City
I think there are no heavens, I think you live
without a sky there. I remember one Sunday
a little girl came out to my house in Raubsville,
Pennsylvania. I don't remember her mother.
The girl was black, the mother was white, after
supper we went outside to look at the sky
and smell the river; the girl was terrified
when she saw the stars; we had to take her inside
and hold her, and love her; she had never seen the sky
except in New York, it was half sad, half horrible.
I remember one night on a hill in Pittsburgh
we tried to look at the stars; we had the charts
in front of us—no one would ever laugh
at either my rages or my fantasies
if he had spent *his* twenty years in Pittsburgh
looking for kindness in that rotten sky.
—My left hand is tying my folder, my right hand is helping.
I am getting ready to leave, I look for
a tip, I touch my hat, I am still living

a little in the age of politeness. I walk
through the cement playground at Sixth and Houston and down
to Vandam Street. My poem is over. My life
is on an even keel, though who's to say
when I will waver again. I start to call
my friends up one at a time to talk about the stars,
my friends on the Upper West Side and my friends in the Village,
my friends in New Jersey and Brooklyn. I listen to them rave,
those poor stargazers, everyone with a story,
everyone either a mystic or a poet,
one a musician, one an astrologer,
all of them illuminated, all of them ecstatic,
every one changed, for a minute, by his own memory.

# RED BIRD

For Greg Pape and Marnie Prange

Now I feel safe,
I've gotten my cardinal back again.
I'm standing in Tuscaloosa,
watching her hop through the puddles.
I'm watching her eat and drink, a brown-chested
queen, living outdoors in sweetness and light
with a loose and rotten sparrow as her playmate,
some common thing not fit to touch her hem,
not fit to live with her in the same puddle.

I have to walk over a sick dog to see them,
and through some bicycles and cardboard boxes.
One has a heavy beak and a scarlet headpiece
and one has ruffled feathers and a black throat.
As long as there is a cardinal in my life
I can go anywhere; she was the bird
that, as it turned out, freed me fifteen years
ago in a town in western Pennsylvania
in some unbearable secret rite involving
a withered pear tree and a patented furnace.
There is a pear tree here too, just to add
a little mistiness, and a truck, and a car,
waiting beside the puddle like two kind horses.
But the cardinal now is sweeter and more whimsical
than the last time, maybe a little smaller, and gentler.
I talk and the sparrow flies away, for God knows
what kind of seed or God knows from what kind of shadow.
Someone will say, as he always does, this sparrow
is English, you know, you have to make a distinction
between him and our own, he is the sloppiest
sparrow of all, he is aggressive and promiscuous,
just as he lands on the pear tree, just as he lands
on the roof of the truck, and someone will say, it is
a female cardinal, the male is redder, his chest
is bigger and brighter, just as she lands on the car
and just as she disappears, a little speck
somewhere, a kind of messenger, her throat
abounding with information, little farewells
to the English sparrow, little bows to the scholars
with bird-stuff on their brains and beautiful cries—
something between a metallic chirp and a whistle—
to the one from Pennsylvania, the one who loves her.

The Jewish King Lear is getting ready
for some kind of horror—he is whispering
in the ears of Regan and Goneril: I know
the past, I know the future, my little hovel

will be in Pennsylvania, I will be
an old man eating from a newspaper,
I will stop to read the news, my fish
will soak the petty world up, it will stretch

from Sears on the left to Gimbels on the right,
my table will be a crate and I will cover
the little spaces with tape, it is enough
for my thin elbows. They will look at him

with hatred reminiscent of the Plains
of Auschwitz—Buchenwald—and drive him mad
an inch at a time. Nothing either in England
or Germany could equal his ferocity,

could equal his rage, even if the Yiddish
could make you laugh. There is a famous picture
of a German soldier plucking a beard; I think
of gentle Gloucester every time I see

that picture. There is a point where even Yiddish
becomes a tragic tongue and even Adler
can make you weep. They sit in their chairs for hours
to hear him curse his God; he looks at the dust

and asks, What have I done, what have I done,
for Him to turn on me; that audience murmurs,
Daughters, daughters, it cries for the sadness that came
to all of them in America. King Lear,

may the Lord keep him, hums in agony,
he is a monster of suffering, so many holes
that he is more like a whistle than like a king,
and yet when sometimes he comes across the stage
.  .  .

crowned with burdocks and nettles and cuckoo flowers
we forget it is Adler, we are so terrified,
we are so touched by pity. It is said
that Isadora Duncan came to worship him,

that John Barrymore came to study his acting,
that when he died they carried his coffin around
from theater to theater, that people mourned in the streets,
that he lay in a Windsor tie and a black silk coat.

One time he carried Cordelia around in his arms
he almost forgot his words, he was so moved
by his own grief, there were tears and groans
for him when they remembered his misfortune.

I thank God they were able to weep
and wring their hands for Lear, and sweet Cordelia,
that it happened almost forty years
before our hell, that there was still time then

to walk out of the theater in the sunlight
and discuss tragedy on the bright sidewalk
and live a while by mercy and innocence
with a king like Adler keeping the tremors alive

in their voices and the tears brimming in their eyes.
Thank God they died so early, that they were buried
one at a time, each with his own service,
that they were not lined up beside the trucks

or the cattle cars. I think when they saw him put
a feather over her lips they were relieved
to see her dead. I think they knew her life
was the last claim against him—the last delusion,

one or two would say. Now he was free,
now he was fully changed, he was *created*,
which is something they could have to talk about
going back to their stairways and their crowded tables
. . .

with real streaks of remorse on their faces—
*more* than forty years, almost fifty,
before the dead were dragged from their places
and dumped on the ground or put in orderly piles—

I think they used a broom on the charred faces
to see if there was breath—and a match or two
was dropped on the naked bodies. For the sake of art
there always was a German or Ukrainian

walking around like a dignified Albany,
or one made sad repentant noises like Kent
and one was philosophical like Edgar,
giving lectures to the burning corpses,

those with gold in their mouths, and those with skin
the color of yellow roses, and those with an arm
or a hand that dropped affectionately on another,
and those whose heads were buried, and those whose black tongues—

as if there were mountains, as if there were cold water
flowing through the ravines, as if there were wine cups
sitting on top of the barrels, as if there were flowers—
still sang in bitterness, still wept and warbled in sorrow.

# THE EXPULSION

I'm working like a dog here, testing my memory,
my mouth is slightly open, my eyes are closed,
my hand is lying under the satin pillow.
My subject is loss, the painter is Masaccio,
the church is the Church of the Carmine, the narrow panel
is on the southwest wall, I make a mouth
like Adam, I make a mouth like Eve, I make
a sword like the angel's. Or Schubert; I hear him howling
too, there is a touch of the Orient
throughout the great C Major. I'm thinking again
of poor Jim Wright and the sheet of tissue paper
he sent me. Lament, lament, for the underlayer
of wallpaper, circa 1935.
Lament for the Cretans, how did they disappear?
Lament for Hannibal. I'm standing again
behind some wires, there are some guns, my hand
is drawing in the eyes, I'm making the stripes,
I'm lying alone with water falling down
the left side of my face. That was our painting.
We stood in line to see it, we loved the cry
that came from Eve's black mouth, we loved the grief
of her slanted eyes, we loved poor Adam's face
half buried in his hands, we loved the light
on the shoulder and thighs, we loved the shadows, we loved
the perfect sense of distance. Lament, lament,
for my sister. It took ten years for the flesh to go,
she would be twenty then, she would be sixty
in 1984. Lament for my father,
he died in Florida, he died from fear, apologizing
to everyone around him. I walked through three feet
of snow to buy a suit; it took a day
to get to the airport. Lament, lament. He had
fifty-eight suits, and a bronze coffin; he lay
with his upper body showing, a foot of carpet.
He came to America in 1905, huge wolves
snapped at the horse's legs, the snow was on the ground
until the end of April. The angel is red,
her finger is pointing, she floats above the gate,
her face is cruel, she isn't like the angels
of Blake, or Plato, she is an angry mother,

her wings are firm. Lament, lament, my father
and I are leaving Paradise, an angel
is shouting, my hand is on my mouth, my father
is on the edge of his bed, he uses a knife
for a shoe horn, he is in Pittsburgh, the sky is black,
the air is filthy, he bends half over to squeeze
his foot into his shoe, his eyes are closed,
he's moaning. I miss our paradise, the pool
of water, the flowers. Our lives are merging, our shoes
are not that different. The angel is rushing by,
her lips are curled, there is a coldness, even
a madness to her, Adam and Eve are roaring,
the whole thing takes a minute, a few seconds,
and we are left on somebody's doorstep, one of
my favorites, three or four marble steps and a simple
crumbling brick—it could be Baltimore,
it could be Pittsburgh, the North Side or the Hill.
Inside I know there is a hall to the left
and a living room to the right; no one has modernized
it yet, there are two plum trees in the back
and a narrow garden, cucumbers and tomatoes.
We talk about Russia, we talk about the garden,
we talk about Truman, and Reagan. Our hands are rubbing
the dusty marble, we sit for an hour. "It is
a crazy life," I say, "after all the model
homes we looked at, I come back to the old
row house, I do it over and over." "My house"—
he means his father's—"had a giant garden
and we had peppers and radishes; my sister
Jenny made the pickles." We start to drift
at 5 o'clock in the evening, the cars from downtown
are starting to poison us. It is a paradise
of two, maybe, two at the most, the name
on the mailbox I can't remember, the garden
is full of glass, there is a jazzy door
on the next house over, and louvered windows. It is
a paradise, I'm sure of it. I kiss
him goodbye, I hold him, almost like the kiss
in 1969, in Philadelphia,
the last time I saw him, in the Russian manner,

his mouth against my mouth, his arms around me—
we could do that once before he died—
the huge planes barely lifting off the ground,
the families weeping beside us, the way they do,
the children waving goodbye, the lovers smiling,
the way they do, all our loss, everything
we know of loneliness there, their minds already
fixed on the pain, their hands already hanging,
under the shining windows, near the yellow tiles,
the secret rooms, the long and brutal corridor
down which we sometimes shuffle, and sometimes run.

# GROUNDHOG LOCK

This is a common plantain, the simple weed
of my solemn childhood, and this is a staghorn sumac,
the weed of my adolescence. I rushed down
to get here before the state got busy pulling
and sawing and cutting. The plantain was our wheat
and it waved in the wind for us; we loved the heads
of tiny green and white flowers, we loved to snap
them loose from the stem and leave them dying there,
for birds, or rabbits, for all we knew. The sumac
was somehow reeking with sex, the branches were covered
with tender velvet and the heavy fruit
was thick with bright red hairs. As I recall
the twigs, when we broke them, had a creamy sap—
we called it milk, or juice—and though the poor shrub
was innocent enough, and no more monstrous
than either the violet or the bitter daisy,
our minds were already ruined.
                            I'm torn between
two stages of my life; the next will be
the stage of silence, of course, and centered around
the sunflower or the hollyhock although
I'm thinking of smoking punk again and sitting
half stoned on nothing under a pussy willow
or a drooping lilac. Maybe I'll live for space
the next time, and practice denial, and sit
on the wooden seesaw and blow the white dandelion
into the river; maybe I'll practice reunion
and pluck the petals: "she loves me, she loves me not,"
a kind of gnosticism; I have ten chances,
sometimes twelve; maybe I'll wait for the milkweed
to come my way, that way I can sit forever
on either the sand or the gravel.
                           There are some steps
going down to the water. I will end my search
on those steps, my own Benares, sixteen risers,
and Budweiser all around me. My last plant
is a morning glory. It comes as if to hide
the chain-link fence, the vine is wrapped around
the heavy wires, a bird is singing, the smell
is more like cotton candy than urine, more

like White Shoulders, there is a dead fish, the flowers
are five to a stem, the leaf is heart-shaped, my arms
can hang between the stone wall and the wire,
my legs can wrap themselves around the roots,
and my back, underneath the neck, the point of exhaustion,
can rest on the worm-like and succulent laterals,
although it could have been a wild carrot
and I could have concentrated on the ivory,
or it could have been the chicory
and I could have concentrated on the blue,
or it could have been crown vetch, there is some
growing on the towpath, I sleep beside it,
three more kinds of existence on the river,
among the picnic tables and the spruce and the pump,
one of the two corners of the universe.

# JULY 2, 1983

This is what it's come to on my primrose path,
a delphinium growing out of a cabbage,
a hosta
or August lily.

This is what a July day looks like
in the 1980's,
a white butterfly,
a shimmer of heat, a shadow.

O ugliest of flowers,
be with me forever,
now that I've lifted my left hand against the tubers,
now that I've lifted my right hand against the motor boats.

O mugho pine,
bless my swallows,
flying madly in and out of their woven duplex,
living for two great weeks with heartbreak and wrangling and terror
and a minute and a half of sleep, and a minute and a half of silence.

# THE DOGS

Sometimes the dogs don't hear me. Sometimes I walk
a mile each way—to the locks and back—singing
a Japanese song, humming a little, remembering
the dry roses. Sometimes I walk through the geese
and they don't move, the guards look up in boredom
and hardly notice, sometimes I see each leaf
is burning from lack of rain, sometimes I reach
the first bridge out of breath, sometimes I rest
in front of the spillway and wait for a breeze. I stand

on the great catwalk, I feel the spray in my face,
I look at the bubbles, I look at the wavering sun,
I look at the winches and wheels, I look at the water
roaring around the bend. There are maples
growing out of the wall, there is giant
purple loosestrife, there are logs and tables,
there are seesaws, there is a well, the lip
is capped, the river is on my left, the sky
is dark and heavy, the island is rich and empty.

# ABOUT THE AUTHOR

GERALD STERN was born in Pittsburgh and educated at the University of Pittsburgh and Columbia University. His books are *The Pineys, Rejoicings, Lucky Life,* and *The Red Coal.* "Father Guzman," a long dramatic poem, was published in *The Paris Review* in 1982. He teaches at The Writers' Workshop at the University of Iowa and lives part of the year there and part of the year in eastern Pennsylvania.

Finding Hope in the Darkness

Christine Driscoll-O'Neill

## Acknowledgments

I would like to thank all the people who inspired this book and helped to bring my story to life.

**To my husband, Jim**. Your love and support have brought me much happiness during the good times and such comfort and strength during the very difficult times. I thank you and want you to know how important you are and always will be to me.

**To the most important person in my life.** Thank you, **God,** for always trying to lead me in the right direction and for all the love you have given me.

**To Richard.** Who was there when I needed him.

**To my employees and friends at One Life at a Time.** Who work hard every day to make a difference.

**To the memory of my parents' teachings**. I was taught to speak up and do the right thing, even if it wasn't popular. I witnessed my parents walking the talk again and again, and that stuck with me over the years.

**To Dina.** Without all your hard work and guidance, this book would not have been possible.

**To Sister Miriam and Sister Lorraine.** I will always be thankful for your support.

**To my friends and family.** I will always love you unconditionally.

**To the most important person in my life. GOD,** Thank you for all of your love and grace.

# Preface

When I reported the pharmaceutical illegal activity to the Federal Government, I had no idea where the complaint would go. I had no way of knowing that the case would so greatly impact my own life but also the lives of people I love and care about deeply.

The company left in its wake many victims — including some doctors and many HIV-positive patients. But in my mind, perhaps the person who lost the most was my brother- in-law, Ben. I had no way of knowing when I submitted my complaint that he would ultimately suffer personally and professionally as a result of the investigation, even though he clearly was never involved in any illegal activities. For that, I will always feel sorry.

Whether it was the work ethic that my dad and mom instilled in me, the need to make my family and friends proud of me, or my drive to be the best I could be, I found that through lots of hard work, I could be successful. That was very important to me, and, in retrospect, it also cost me. My desire for success made work so important to me.

When my confidence and self-esteem were threatened, and my life was crumbling all around me, I thought that perhaps my earlier success had just been a fluke. Perhaps my siblings and friends had been right.

Only when times were difficult, when my business and work were no longer thriving, did I come to understand who I really was and how far I had come from my childhood, my difficult teens, and all the secrets and pain that I had carried for far too long.

I would learn that I wouldn't allow those dark times to define me. Instead, they would push me to succeed again and again. I feel most proud that I have survived so many losses and thrived. By having faith, hope, and a great support network over the years, I've been able to get back up when I've been knocked down.

Through all the challenges and rewards, I have been brought to a greater truth and life purpose, and that has been the greatest gift of this journey.

# Contents

## Introduction

## I Had to Make Things Right

I felt rage — pure, unadulterated rage — bubbling up inside me.

I was on the phone with a science liaison at the pharmaceutical company I was working for, and I couldn't believe what I was hearing. The liaison was telling me, in the most casual tone, that the drug study I had put dozens of AIDS patients through had not been authorized by the federal government. My supervisor had set up the false study to make money. The liaison told me that the company planned to halt the study immediately and would inform the patients and their doctor.

"Just come back to the main office, Chris," the liaison said. "I will tell the doctors and patients that we need to stop the study."

But this liaison didn't know any of these patients. She hadn't laughed with them in high moments and cried with them in low moments. She didn't know how brave some of them were, or how broken some felt as they faced their own mortality.
She didn't see how much better the drug made some feel and how much pain it caused others. She hadn't gone to dinner with them, held their trembling hands, or listened to their relationship troubles.

She hadn't walked through this deadly disease with them like I had.

As the science liaison talked about suddenly halting a drug study that patients were depending on, I was stunned into silence for a moment, my throat suddenly dry. The faces of the patients I had worked with for several months scrolled through my mind like a movie running in slow motion.

"I don't understand. How could this happen?" I asked. "We can't just take the drug away from the patients. They're depending on it to get better. We can't do this to them."

"It's OK. I'll take care of it," the liaison said in a way that made her sound already tired of the conversation.

"No, you won't," I told her. "I will stay with the patients. I will talk to them. And I will take care of this myself."

Believe me, I was not naïve. I knew some of my fellow sales representatives would do just about anything to make a profit on Serostim, a drug that helped prevent AIDS patients' organs from deteriorating, or wasting, as it's called. I had been in meetings with other reps and managers, and I had watched them offer doctors cash in exchange for prescribing the drug. I knew it was wrong. I knew they were bribing doctors in an effort to pump up company drug business — and line their own pockets with plenty of commission cash.

It all rubbed me the wrong way, and I had complained to company officials about it. Company executives had always justified this behavior, pointing out that the drug was truly helping people get better. It was prolonging people's lives, and they were right about that. I was seeing the proof with my own eyes in the faces of the patients. So I had tried to tell myself, that if the company and some of the doctors were profiting from a drug that made people suffer less, maybe the good outweighed the bad.

But now, this was altogether different. The company I was working for directed me to give patients high doses of this expensive and powerful drug. Those high doses had caused all kinds of side effects, including severe pain. Some of the patients had so much pain that they had trouble walking. And this study hadn't been authorized?

My discovery that the study was a sham would be the beginning of a very difficult journey with a company and patients that were more than just a job.

This was all about making money?

## My Story

I'm Chris Driscoll-O'Neill, and this is my story.

In order to understand why I made that frantic phone call that turned not only my life but others' lives upside down, you need to know what drives me. And so, I invite you, my reader, to glimpse into my life—into my painful struggles—in order to understand why doing the right thing is so very important to me. It has not always been easy, and I have not always made popular decisions.

## Faith, Hope, and Love

I'm sharing my story, the successes and the failures, the proud moments and the painful moments, in the hope of helping anyone who struggles with loss and feels alone. I believe that everyone is tested—whether it's through the loss of a child, parent, spouse, job, a divorce, or personal relationship. It's just part of life, and it can rattle you to your core.

I also believe God has a big plan for everyone. I've learned that I'm at my best when I listen to my heart and follow where he leads me. My life has more meaning when God is with me. When I couldn't find God, I went into despair and lost hope and found him again in the darkest place a soul can endure and still survive. It was in those darkest moments that I faced the secrets and trauma that had haunted me for years.

For all those that have lost hope, may you find the needed strength to remain positive when times are tough! May you choose to see the silver lining in difficult times, and remember to always get back up when life knocks you down.

One last thing: don't be afraid to feel your pain and ask for help when you need a friend to lean on. Life is short. You deserve to be happy.

And so my life story begins...

# In the Beginning

# Chapter One: From Humble Beginnings

## My Parents

I grew up in an Irish Catholic home. Both my dad and my mom were 100 percent Irish Catholic and from large families. My dad was one of eight children; my mom was one of nine children.

Like my parents' families, we were a big family, the nine of us. My parents would have done without to give their seven children everything we needed.

My dad was in the navy, so he was gone for long stretches of time and came home for brief visits—just long enough to produce another sibling. Most of us were born a year or less apart.

Looking back on my early childhood, I suppose we were considered lower middle class, although at the time, I didn't know any different or long for any more than we had. Money certainly wasn't free-flowing, but we were well fed, and we had all the necessities, including new clothes at the beginning of every school year.

We lived in three small apartments in three different Boston, Massachusetts, housing projects. D Street projects and Third Street and finally Columbia Point project. Initially, our tiny apartment had probably about several hundred square feet, as our family grew, our parents found a way to pay a little more for a slightly bigger place with three bedrooms. But for a family of nine, even the largest apartment felt cramped.

We had only one bathroom; my parents had one bedroom; my three brothers had another; and the four of us girls shared the third, with two of us squeezing into two twin beds. I shared a bed with my older sister Carly, so we each slept at opposite ends of the bed, with my feet in her face and her feet in mine. Sometimes I'd grab my pillow and blanket and curl up on the floor instead — just for a little extra space.

Other families in the housing projects depended on welfare checks to pay their bills and got their Christmas delivered by the Salvation Army. My dad was adamant that his family would never go on welfare.

"You can get anything you want if you work hard enough," he used to say. "Things in life don't always come easily, but that's life. If you keep working hard, it will pay off."

And no matter how tight our money was, my parents also found a way to splurge a little at Christmas time. They gave us bicycles some years; other times, they gave all the girls sewing machines. I suspect that, at times, my parents may have even taken out loans to make Christmas special for us.

Aside from material possessions, I always felt we were lucky in other ways. Many of my friends' dads were either never in the picture or had long abandoned their families, leaving the mothers to raise the children alone. Some of my friends' mothers took up company with a series of so-called uncles — guys who hung around just long enough to make the kids think that maybe they'd stay for the long haul, but then they'd disappear just as quickly as they had dropped in. Or in some cases, these guys were either dismissive or mean to the kids, and when they were gone, the children breathed a sigh of relief — until the next uncle came along.

In contrast, my parents were still married—happily so—and even if my dad was away a lot with the military, I felt secure knowing he wanted to be with us. I could count on him coming back, no matter what.

## Family Dynamics

I was the second oldest and one of four girls in the family, sandwiched in birth order between my older sister, Carly, and my younger sister, Lisa. The two of them were tight and played together often, but for whatever reason, I never meshed well with them. I got the impression at a very early age that they didn't like me very much.

I was shy, and I spent a lot of time feeling somewhat uneasy in my own home among some of my siblings. In a family of seven children, I was the oddball; I guess you might say I was the black sheep, the child who never quite fit in with the rest, especially with my sisters who were closest in age to me.

## Finding God

I searched for a long time to be loved and to love someone. I always felt that God was a strong presence in my life even as a child. I always felt close to God and found peace in church. I liked to sit in church and talk to God. I thought, *I could tell God anything and he would understand and still love me, no matter what.* "I never ever remember not loving God, my Father."

## Early School Years

I started kindergarten early, before age five, and I always had trouble focusing in school. The teachers rattled on, and I daydreamed, staring out the classroom window and wishing I was anywhere else but there. So when it came time to do the work, I was a little lost because I hadn't paid any attention.

In first grade, my teacher was concerned and asked my mom to visit the classroom to observe my behavior. My mother didn't tell me she was coming. She just quietly slipped into the room, sat at a desk near the back of the room, and watched me. She stayed most of the day, and I had no idea she was even there. I was so busy doing my thing—staring out the window, getting lost in my thoughts—that I never even noticed her.

Near the end of that first grade year, my mother came into my bedroom and sat on the edge of the bed next to me.

"Chris, we're going to have you repeat first grade," she said gently. "But don't worry—it's not a bad thing. You'll be in a classroom with more children your own age. It will be better."

But I felt she was only trying to put a good spin on this troubling news. I saw it only as a failure, and I worried about being ridiculed. I remembered a little girl who had been forced to repeat kindergarten; other kids made fun of her, looked down on her, and called her stupid.

I cried and begged to move to second grade with the other kids.

"I'll try harder," I pleaded. "I'll do better, I promise! Please let me move on to second grade!"

But the decision had clearly been made, and although my mother comforted me, she didn't budge. At the very same time I wasn't cutting it in first grade, Carly's teacher was recommending her for a double promotion, because she was sailing through school.

*I must be stupid,* I thought. And for many years, that's how I saw myself: dumb.

I continued daydreaming, and I often had trouble focusing on finishing one task before starting another. I had a very hard time sitting still at my desk and listening to a teacher talk for long periods. I would tell myself to listen, but my mind would drift off and my body would grow antsy, longing to move. This not only frustrated my teachers and parents, but it also frustrated and exhausted me.

Yet, despite my mind's tendency to wander and my body's resistance to sitting still, I was determined to do well, and I worked hard. In some ways, I probably worked harder than other classmates who didn't seem to have any trouble keeping their minds and bodies in place. I thought something was wrong with me.

And actually, something was wrong with me, but it wasn't that I was stupid—an IQ test I took as an adult finally convinced me that I had average, if not above average, intelligence. Instead, I had—and still have—Attention Deficit Disorder (ADD), also referred to as ADHD.

Back then, it went undiagnosed.

I attended a girl's school in Boston for most of elementary school. The school was within walking distance of our home. I would either walk with my older sisters or schoolmates. If money hadn't been an issue for my parents, I would have loved to have attended Catholic school (grades one through twelve).

## Not Feeling Good about Myself

I always felt so different from my sisters. They were the pretty ones—strikingly so, even as young girls—and I was not. I recall one of my aunts making a comment, more than once, within earshot: "Chris is not that pretty, but she has a good personality." She said it in this matter-of-fact way, but her words hit me hard in the gut. *I'm not pretty?* It hadn't occurred to me that I wasn't as attractive as my siblings until I heard her say that. And from that point on, I would stare at myself in the mirror and think about all the things I would like to change about my appearance, things that might make me prettier like my sisters.

I actually did have a decent personality. Family members said I was always outgoing and friendly, usually happy and agreeable as a young child. In school, I always had friends and laughed a lot. I wasn't the class clown; I was just a happy, fun kid.

## Moving to the Suburbs

During the summer before sixth grade, my family moved from the inner-city housing projects to a sleepy suburb about thirty miles south of Boston, Massachusetts.

When I asked why, my parents said that it was time to move out of the area; they were concerned with the increased racial tension in the housing projects. Later, I would learn they moved because they feared for the family's safety. For the first time in all the years they had lived in the city, they heard stories of young girls being attacked and raped. Suddenly, other parents were engaged in fistfights outside our apartment.

One benefit of moving to the suburbs was space. Our new three- bedroom house had a basement and a big back yard. It was huge compared to our previous apartment. The town was quiet and country-like with plenty of undeveloped land — it was nothing like the bustling city we were used to.

In the housing projects, most of my friends had been Black, so it was strange to suddenly live in a town where most residents were white. And I had always attended an all-girls school in Boston, but here I was, on the verge of puberty, going to a public school — with boys.

Throughout my remaining school years, I made some friends, but I was generally shy and reserved. When someone would say something nice about my personality, I never took it well. I was sure that he or she really meant that I wasn't pretty, not to mention a little chunky.

Carly and Lisa were outgoing, pretty, and popular; Lisa had even been her class prom queen. Trust me; both of my sisters were beautiful enough and popular enough to be prom queens.
However, unlike my sisters, I was not pencil thin, and I guess that's what boys wanted — girls that were pretty and thin.

It's tough enough to be around beautiful people when you've been told you are not beautiful. But when your sisters are those beautiful people, and you are constantly surrounded by them—it's beyond tough when you don't feel you measure up.

I was popular with the girls all through school. My classmates even voted me friendliest, and I got second place for best personality.
Yet I felt I still didn't measure up, but I didn't know why, and I started to overeat and purge, because I felt guilty. Yes I am a bulimic.

Purging was a way to gain some control of my life, but it would also contribute to later physical effects—stomach and esophageal reflux. I was interested in boys, but I didn't date in high school, largely because the guys didn't pay attention to me—unless it was to get closer to my sisters. A guy once became friendly with me in school by joking around with me in class. Just when I started wondering if he might like me, he leaned in, and I knew an important question was coming. My heart was pounding with excitement.

"Do you think you could fix me up with your sister, Lisa?" he asked in a low voice.

"Oh," I said, looking away, hoping my face wasn't red, hoping it wouldn't reveal my surprise and disappointment. "You like Lisa?"

"Well yeah," the boy said. "I do. Do you think she might like me? Do you think she might go out with me?"

I smiled at him. This boy was so eager for Lisa to like him; my heart went out to him in a way. I knew exactly how he felt, I will let you know. I will talk to her,"I promised.

So I told Lisa about the boy in my grade—he was a little younger— and she did indeed agree to go out with him.

I fell for the same thing other times when guys seemed interested in me—at least, I got so caught up in little bit of attention they paid me that I assumed they liked me. But sooner or later, it was clear that they were really after Lisa or Carly. I often acted as the go- between for my sisters and these boys.

I felt somewhat invisible during that time, even among the girls in my class. Kids in my own grade would say to Carly, "I didn't know you had a younger sister. What does she look like?" And this would be a girl who attended all the same classes that I did.

I ended up earning decent grades, despite a rough start in my early school years. My grades were high enough in high school to make the honor roll. But still, no matter how well I did in school, it didn't matter. I still thought something was wrong with me.

Years of feeling second to my sisters and classmates— especially Carly, who had excelled in school while I had struggled—coupled with my sisters' beauty and my poor self-image would hurt me for decades.

I was a people pleaser, and I learned to hide my feelings to protect myself. When people said hurtful things to me, I took it all in and didn't retaliate.

## Doing the Right Thing

After my family moved to the suburbs, my dad went into semi- retirement from the military, and although he continued to work as a machinist, he was home every night. I had always looked up to my dad. His family was everything to him, and I knew he worked hard to provide for us. He was intent on instilling a strong work ethic in his children, as well as the unshakable moral compass he lived by. This work ethic would stick with me over the years.

My dad was plugged in politically and threw his support wholeheartedly behind candidates he believed in. He also showed us that he was willing to take on anyone — any establishment — to fight for what was right. When my dad learned that a Catholic priest was molesting a young person close to the family, my dad hit the roof. My dad was a deeply religious man who leaned heavily on his faith and was involved with the church, getting close to the priests and other leaders there. We had so little money, and yet he always dropped a few dollars or some change — whatever he could spare — into the collection baskets every Sunday.

Despite his strong alliance with the church, my dad was incensed that this priest had hurt a child, and he took it upon himself to write to the Archdiocese of Boston and request that this abusive priest be removed from our church. I sensed that his rocking the boat put my dad in an awkward position with local church officials who likely questioned why he would rat on one of his own. But my dad refused to apologize and held his head high, sure that he was doing the right thing and that he had God on his side. And in fact, within a short period, this questionable priest did indeed quietly disappear from our parish.

I was in awe of my dad, filled with pride that he had spoken up to correct a wrong, even though it meant confronting an institution he'd supported wholeheartedly and stepping on the egos of people in positions of authority. I wanted to believe that I had that same strength of character, and that if I was ever faced with the same kind of crossroads—speaking up or looking the other way—I would do the right thing, just as my dad had done, even if it wasn't easy

or comfortable for me. Be careful what you wish for—I did indeed inherit this particular personality trait from my dad, and it would prove to be my Achilles' heel.

## Difficult Teen Years

And yet, despite my admiration for my dad, we had a complicated relationship during my teen years. While he had been away in the military, I had longed to have him home. He had been gone for so long, dropping in from the navy for brief visits. But now that he was home all the time, I didn't like it, and I had a tough time adjusting to his constant presence.

He was suddenly shouting orders and doling out discipline— something he was probably used to doing as a chief petty officer in the navy. But I was stubborn and resisted his orders. They didn't sit well with me, and so my dad and I clashed hard. There were also periods when he was out of work, and I could sense that money was tight and that my parents were worried about losing the house.

My dad treated my sisters differently. At family gatherings, he would talk proudly about Carly and Lisa, gushing about how beautiful they were and that they were both dating football quarterbacks. In fact, Lisa ended up marrying her quarterback boyfriend, a guy name Ben. But my dad didn't talk in that same soft tone about me. He didn't like my friends. He sensed that I was different from my sisters—and not in a way he liked. He was tough on me. I'm sure he probably loved me, but in those years, he didn't show me any affection or express his love in words. I wanted him to feel that same sense of pride in me that he felt in my sisters, but deep in my heart, I felt that I would never measure up to my sisters in my dad's eyes. At the time, I didn't have it in me to compete with them, either.

I don't want to make it sound like I was completely innocent. I definitely misbehaved and gave him reasons to get angry with me.

"I'm taking the car, Dad," I would say. "I'll be right back." But then I would stay out for way too long, and he would give me heck for it. And when my dad tried to straighten me out and tell me what to do, I would open my mouth and talk back to him.

"You can't tell me what to do!" I'd shout. "I'll do what I want!"

We both said things that we probably wished we could take back. At times my dad lashed out in hurtful ways. He called me "stupid"—a word he probably knew hit a nerve with me—and he punished my disobedience harshly, grounding me or even giving me a hard punch in the arm or a slap of the belt every now and then.

"Teresa," I would overhear him saying to my mother, "Chris always has to learn everything the hard way. What are we going to do with her?"

He told my mother I reminded him of his sister, who had a reputation in the family for being a lively, outspoken firecracker. But to my dad, that type of behavior was not something to be proud of. My mom was protective of me, but she also tried not to get in the middle of our battles. She used to come to me after a fight and smooth my hair back.

"Your dad worries about you because you're actually so much like him," she would say gently. "You're sensitive and naïve and you wear your heart on your sleeve — just like he does." But it felt like he wanted to beat the wild out of me, and all I wanted to do was rebel against his attempts to tame me. The harder he cracked down, the more I bucked; and the more I bucked, the tougher he got.

It didn't help that I also had a certain knack for getting caught when I did something wrong. My siblings certainly didn't behave perfectly. But it seemed that I was always the one whose behavior got noticed — and then punished.

## Last Straw for Dad

Once, when I was sixteen, my younger sister Lisa, a friend, and I were getting ready to go to a school dance, and we started drinking some booze that Lisa had gotten from someone old enough to buy it. My friend was drinking from the bottle in public, right in front of a liquor store. Police officers arrived, catching us all off guard.

"Do you girls have any identification?" one of the officers asked us. We stared back at him.

I was the only one with a driver's license, so for some reason I was the one taken to jail and the other girls were let go. I watched my sister and the other girl run off. The police never arrested me, but they took me into the station and told me I had to call my parents.

My mom answered the phone. "If you tell Dad, I'm not coming back home," I told my mom, fearful of my dad's reaction.

I knew my mother wasn't going to keep something like that from him. And as it turned out, it was the final straw for my worried dad.

"We're sending you to your cousin, Penny's house in a Massachusetts suburb for the summer," he told me soon afterward. "I think if you spend the summer there, you can work on some things. I think you will come back a better person."

At first I was upset about it and felt cast out. It was far enough from my home that I couldn't hang out with my friends.
Without a car, I really was stuck with my relatives. But it turned out to be a good thing for me. I would help my aunt and make new friends. I didn't have to compete with my sisters, and it was a relief to get away from my dad for a while. I enjoyed Penny's company and liked watching her kids—and most of all; I could just be myself and relax.

By the end of the summer, I felt a boost in my confidence. I was close to graduating high school by this point, so I knew I wouldn't be living with my parents much longer. The rest of my time at home went more smoothly. My grades went up, and my dad and I learned to live with each other and clashed less often. I came to understand that if he was hard on me, it was because he wanted me to be better, more responsible, and more focused on doing the right thing.

## Rebellious Years

I knew my dad was right about my social behavior at times. I was rebellious, and every time I was compared to one of my dad's sisters, an aunt, it seemed more likes a compliment to me than an insult. My dad's sisters were fun and considered wild, but that intrigued me. Being so shy and unable to control my feelings of not being good enough, I wished that I could be more like them.

I knew but didn't realize, until I had more maturity under my belt, that my wild spirit came from my dad's sisters and did not resemble my mom and sisters. This wildness created a lot of conflict for my mom. She understood that I felt different and knew, as mothers often do, that I was somewhat lost, and not in a good way.

I wish we had talked more then, but I had pain and secrets that I didn't know what to do with. And unfortunately, my family was like most—we didn't talk about our feelings, our problems, or our issues.

So I medicated myself, with alcohol mostly and some drugs. By the grace of God, I was sensitive or allergic to narcotics or hard drugs. I experimented but I never got hooked or dependent on drugs like some of my friends did. My insecurities would only go from bad to worse, thanks to a night that went terribly wrong.

## On My Own

I didn't go straight to college after graduating from high school. Instead, I worked first as a phlebotomist but without formal training. The work didn't pay all that well—about three hundred dollars a week—but I loved interacting with patients.

Not long after high school graduation, I moved out of my parents' home to an apartment in the suburbs of Massachusetts, a city approximately twenty-five miles south of Boston and thirty miles northeast of Providence, Rhode Island. Two of my women friends from the hospital had suggested I move in with them.

At first my parents were concerned, but they also knew their life would be less stressful with me out of the house. I quickly learned that playing house had a real serious downside—bills. With freedom came rent, utilities, groceries, etc. Paying my parents money for room and board sure looked a lot better after I left.

Even with two roommates, money was tight. I could sense when I called my parents or stopped by to visit that they were really enjoying my new reality. Don't think I didn't entertain surrendering to my dad's rules to save a few dollars and live a little, but I guess I was too stubborn to admit defeat.

I had always appreciated the sacrifices my parents had endured for their family, but until you're on your own, you really can't wrap your head around the anxiety of wondering whether the money will stretch far enough to pay the bills.

On more than one occasion, eating well was not an option if rent was due later that week. At times, even fast food was too expensive. I knew even God was getting a kick out of my new freedom.

An older car meant insurance; a newer car meant car payments and more insurance. The bills never seemed to end. I worked hard and always whined about having to pay bills. I preferred to spend my paycheck on fun things, or to go out and enjoy life. I still whine about bills.

My roommates were party girls and that appealed to me. I was responsible enough to get up for work and do my job, but partying made me feel numb. Every time unpleasant memories or events occurred, I just washed them away with my new friends. The best part was I thought I was so smart — that my family didn't know what I was up to.

Leaving home at that time, without confronting my demons, was the worst thing I could have done, and I'm glad my parents didn't know just how much I partied. I was distancing myself from everyone by using lots of alcohol to medicate my pain.

### Teen Bride

While at a bar in Newport, Rhode Island, with friends, I glanced over and noticed a guy — Bob — trying to catch my eye. He kept winking at me. But I saw that he was with another girl, so I quickly looked away. When I went into the ladies room, he followed me inside.

"Hi there. What's your name?" he asked.

"I'm Chris. But—you're in the ladies room," I said a little shyly. I giggled in spite of myself.

Bob ended up following my friends and me home that night, all the way from Newport, Rhode Island, to my apartment in southern Massachusetts. After that, he started coming over to my place all the time.

He seemed like a great guy at first. He was a social worker with a master's degree; he was handsome, sweet, and charming. And most importantly, he was the first guy I had ever met who wasn't interested in my sisters or my friends; he was interested in me and me alone, and that made me feel special.

We hadn't been dating long when Bob began asking me to marry him. I wasn't ready at first. I was only eighteen, and I didn't feel I knew him all that well. So I put him off, but he kept asking. He wrote me a sappy note.

"I can't live without you, Chris," he wrote. "I'll do anything for you. We could even move to England and you could start that singing career you've always dreamed of."

I probably should have known from the first time I met Bob that he was not the best match for me. My friends liked him; they thought he was charismatic and cute. But my family saw another side of him, a controlling side. Still, I disregarded my family's concerns, still being rebellious I decided to be in control and marry him anyway.

18

And when Bob continued to propose pretty much every day, he finally wore me down until I said yes. I had only known him a matter of weeks. At the time, I thought I loved him, but looking back, I was probably more in love with the thought that someone seemed to love me.

At one point, Bob's mother called my mother to say that she felt our upcoming marriage was a bad idea. I was too young, she said. And besides, Bob and I came from different backgrounds, which meant that his family had money and mine did not. But I was annoyed that Bob's mother was meddling, and at the time, it only strengthened my resolve to marry Bob.

The wedding, which was held over Labor Day weekend in 1970— just three months after Bob and I had met—was a grand affair with about three hundred people in attendance. While I was in the limousine with my dad on the way to the church, I suddenly panicked and felt overwhelmed by second thoughts.

"I don't want to marry him," I quietly confessed to my dad.

I thought he might tell me I didn't have to go through with it, that we could keep driving right past that church, then I could start over. And if he was behind me, I knew I would have the strength to call the wedding off. But my dad brushed off my apprehension.

"You can't say that now," he told me. It seemed he was more concerned with how a fleeing bride at the altar would look to our many friends and relatives.

And so I took a deep breath, tried to convince myself it was just wedding day jitters, and decided I needed to see this through.

The ceremony was held at a Catholic church, and the reception was at a fancy and expensive party hall in the city. The day was lovely, and I tried to enjoy the party and brush aside all my doubts.

But just a day later, during our honeymoon in Florida, I broke down crying. I knew I had made the wrong decision, and the force of it hit me hard. I couldn't hide my despair from Bob.

"I don't think this is what I want in my life right now," I said. "C'mon," he said. "Let's just give it a shot."

### Early in the Marriage

I decided that I would do just that, but the marriage was rocky from the start. We moved to Rhode Island to live in his aunt's double-decker home, but we didn't have enough money for a phone or any furniture. I was working two jobs, while Bob remained unemployed.

One day, Bob's aunt got a phone message from his old girlfriend and relayed it to me, so I began to suspect that he was having an affair with at least one other woman, maybe more. He was also on edge quite often, his anger burning just below the surface.

Before long, he began treating me differently—cruelly.

We moved to Rhode Island, and I made friends easily. We were living in a small studio apartment, again without any furniture.

One night I came home from work with a pizza with anchovies, and he was so disgusted by the anchovies that he threw the hot pizza in my face. Later, while Bob was still unemployed, he slipped a couple hits of acid into my candy bar and didn't tell me until after I had eaten it. I tried to focus on watching the Miss America pageant on TV, but the women looked like they were melting, and I felt as though I had no teeth.

I was scared and started freaking out. "What did you do?" I asked.

"It was supposed to be a fun thing, to make you relax," he said.

"Bob, I don't feel well," I told him. "I think I should go to the emergency room."

"I'm not taking you to the hospital," he said. "I might get in trouble if they found out what I did. You'll be OK. Just wait it out."

I couldn't believe he had done that to me.

## Marriage Is on the Rocks

Bob couldn't find work as a social worker, and the idea of being a police officer appealed to him. Not long after getting a job as a police officer, Bob began getting more physical when he got angry with me, grabbing me by the arm and squeezing hard. One night when we had friends over, Bob started tripping me when I walked by him, and after our friends left, he suddenly ran after me in attack mode. I tried locking myself into the bathroom, but he punched through the door and beat me in the face with his fists.

I sat at the bottom of the stairs leading to our attic apartment, crying, not knowing what to do. I couldn't go home to my parents. How could I admit that I was unhappy, that my marriage was awful? I felt like a failure. The next day came, and I had bruises around my eyes. He said he was sorry, and I tried to let it go.

As tough as the physical abuse was, the cruel things he said and did were even tougher. He would purposely give me blouses that were the wrong size for Christmas, then take them back and give me nothing in exchange.

And he would often tear me down, comparing me to his female friends by saying, "You're not a woman. You don't have breasts like my friends."

Or he would tell me I looked like my mother and already had lines on my face. Since my self-esteem was already super low, I took it all to heart and believed every word. That feeling of inadequacy had haunted me since the first time someone had said I wasn't pretty.

I let him control me. Bob tried to keep me away from my family. When an uncle died, I wanted to attend the funeral, but Bob took apart the car's carburetor to prevent me from going.

"If your family wants you to go, they'll come get you," he told me. I ended up calling family members and making excuses for not attending.

Sometimes he would take me to a bar and shamelessly flirt with other women in front of me. At times, he would make bets with guys that he could get another girl's phone number while I was there watching—and he did.

I didn't stand up for myself. I let him do all of this to me. Before we went to a party, if he said something to me about how unattractive I looked, I would sit in a corner all night by myself. Bob even told me at one point that if he had known that I had been left back in the first grade, he never would have married me.

My mother had been right. Don't tell men much about your history; they could use it later to hurt you.

I just wanted to be loved. But after so much emotional and physical abuse, and public humiliation, I knew Bob and I didn't really love each other.

Bob worked an overnight shift then, and at times he came home drunk. I suspected he was having an affair with a coworker, a female police officer. One day, about five years into the marriage, he came home and told me, "I love you, but I can't live with you," and he started moving the television and other things from the house into his girlfriend's place.

Bob's mother told me that Bob would agree to go to counseling with me if I signed over all the stocks we owned together.
Hanging onto hope that we could make the marriage work, I signed the papers, but Bob still refused to see a counselor. He even took my car, a brand-new Volkswagen, from the parking lot at work, all without saying a word to me. I walked out to the parking lot after work one day, and my car was gone. I knew he had taken it.

I had been the breadwinner, but he took everything we had in savings and everything we owned together. I was left with nothing.

## Family Heart Issues

Around this time, my mother had a heart attack, and my family was reeling from that. At first, I didn't feel like I could tell my family about my marital troubles. Besides, I didn't want to admit I had failed. I sat stunned in my apartment, all alone, with almost nothing left.

Then my dad had a heart attack, and shortly afterward, I did tell him that Bob had left me.

"Please, whatever you do, make him take you back," my dad pleaded. He was sick and wanted to believe everything would be OK.

I knew I couldn't beg Bob to take me back; I knew the marriage was over. Eventually, my dad understood that, and he started making arrangements for an annulment.

But then he suffered more heart trouble and was admitted to a local hospital south of Boston. When I showed up for a visit, some my siblings started telling me that I shouldn't see him, because my failing marriage was causing my dad stress he didn't need.

I went to see him anyway.

"Take care of the family," my dad said to me when I was alone with him in the hospital room.

"I will," I promised. I was touched that he saw something in me, maybe the same protective nature he had, that told him I could help keep the family together.

Not long afterward, in the summer of 1975, my dad died.

## Double Loss

The double loss of my marriage and my dad floored me. I felt as if I was in a daze. When they closed the casket at my dad's funeral, grief overwhelmed me. I didn't want my dad to leave. There were so many things I wished I could have said and done differently. I didn't have a chance to tell my dad that I would be OK. I wanted him to see that. And I wanted him to know that everything he taught me about taking the high road and doing the right thing had made a difference in my life. I wanted to tell him I was so sorry for being rebellious and apologize for all the hurtful things I had said over the years.

And more than anything, I wanted to tell him I needed him and loved him.

With nowhere to live, I toyed with the idea of moving in with my mother for a short period, figuring I could recover from my divorce, and my mom and I could comfort each other in the wake of my dad's death. But my brothers told me they didn't think it was a good idea, and instead, they moved in to help my mother. In fact, some family members told me they blamed me for causing my dad's death that the stress of my dissolving marriage had done him in.

At the time, I believed I was to blame and carried the weight of that guilt for many years. I was hurting, too, but it seemed that my family felt no sympathy for me.

I felt a deep sense of rejection. Once again, I was the outcast in the family.

## Feeling Lost

Reeling from the loss of my dad and the dissolution of my marriage all at once, I felt lost.

I moved back into an apartment with my two former roommates, and for several months, I found myself drifting with these women into a world of heavy drinking and sleeping around — there was a professor, a psychologist, and a man several years my junior.

I had sex with different men, because I could. I was so badly scarred from my husband. I didn't want to get attached to anyone, and I didn't have any respect for men. I regarded them with cold detachment, believing I could love them and leave them without any problem.

In some ways, I hated men, and I wanted to hurt them. It made me feel like, "Aha! I have the power!"

But that sense of satisfaction never lasted long. It was a flattering thing. I would feel good about loving and leaving them, and then on the ride home, I would start feeling awful. Sometimes after being with a man, I would start crying — not only out of grief for my dad but also for my horrible marriage. After partying one night with my roommates and sleeping with a guy, I woke up the next morning, and realized I barely recognized myself.

I freaked out. I realized that I had had a lot to drink and I had probably acted like an ass the night before. I suddenly woke up to the way I had been behaving for a while, and I felt embarrassed and ashamed. I looked at my roommates and knew I didn't want to end up like them. They lived from drink to drink and man to man.

Snow was coming down hard that February day, but I couldn't wait for the weather to clear. I gathered my things together and moved out right away, cutting ties with both women. I learned later that one of them had straightened out her life, and the other one hadn't.

I moved in with an aunt at first and later found my own place. I began dating a man for a couple of years, but I was still suffering inside, feeling low about myself. I felt like I needed some space to figure out who I was, so I moved down to Sarasota Florida for about eighteen months.

I needed to go away and get my life together. No one knew me there, so I felt like I could pick up and start over.

While there, I immersed myself in counseling and worked though my self-esteem issues. I learned that I had trouble with relationships, because I was unable to trust anyone. At times, I felt so completely alone. When my husband left me and my dad died, I thought there was no one I could turn to. I didn't feel as if I could talk to my mother then, because she was going through her own grief, and I didn't want to worry her. And my siblings and I never talked about personal troubles in that way.

I started to realize that I needed to be strong, independent, and self-reliant. I needed to get through that difficult time on my own.
For the first time in a long time, with the help of therapy, I sensed my self-esteem rising. My boyfriend had followed me down to Florida and asked me to marry him, but he was also involved in drugs. I knew in my heart that the relationship wasn't right, and I turned him away. I wasn't ready to marry anybody — not then — and I had grown up enough to know that I had to say no.

## Meeting Jim

After living in Florida for more than a year, my mother started having health problems, and I returned to Massachusetts. Around this time, I met Jim—the man who would later become my husband.

He left a note on my car in a college parking lot that said, "You're cute. Would you like to meet for coffee?"

I was dating someone else, but I had a good feeling about Jim, so I agreed to meet with him. We talked and laughed and had a good time.

"You have a great smile," Jim told me. I searched his face, wondering if he was for real. After all, I wasn't used to hearing compliments from men. But he wasn't giving me a line. He was telling me the truth as he saw it.

It didn't take long for me to see that Jim was different from anyone else I had ever dated. He was soft-spoken, kind, and gentle. He was honest. The more I got to know him, the more I liked him. He was dependable. If I was looking awful or was having a bad day, it didn't matter to him. He was there for me. I felt in my heart that he would always be there, no matter what.

We had been dating for about a year when Jim got down on one knee and said, "Will you marry me?" He produced a beautiful diamond ring.

I was in love with Jim, and I was tempted, but I had been burned before. I couldn't say yes in that moment. I was too scared.

"Can we call this a friendship ring for now?" I asked. "I need to take things slow."

"OK," he said. "I do believe you're worth the wait."

# Chapter Two: Life before Serostim

## Founding a Medical Lab Business in the Early 1980s

Despite loving the hospital work, the pay wasn't that great. Eventually, I realized I needed to find a way to make more money.

This became clear after I slipped on some wet steps and broke my tailbone. I was laid up for several weeks, and during that time I didn't get paid a cent, because my employer didn't have the necessary insurance to cover my injury.

It also occurred to me that I needed to make more money because my sister Donna might need my help with money someday. Donna had given birth to a child with multiple deformities and was struggling financially. *The jobs I'd held would never allow me to help her and her family.*

A desire to earn more money pushed me to make the somewhat radical decision to start my own medical lab business with a friend in the early 1980s. It started out as a far-fetched idea, something we joked about as a means to being our own bosses, but I quickly got excited about the prospect and began putting plans together.

Getting started wasn't easy, though. We must have seemed like a risky venture, because we couldn't convince any banks to give us a large loan. "I'm sorry; you don't qualify," bankers told me over and over.

"Why?" I asked. "I have excellent credit."

"You're asking for a large chunk of money, and you don't have experience with owning your own business," they told me. "But how do I get that experience if I don't get help with my first business venture?" I asked.

No one seemed to have an answer for that. I tried several different banks, but I received one rejection after another.

So I went to three different banks and got approved for three small, personal loans, each for three thousand dollars. With that small amount of seed money, I opened the medical lab south of Boston in 1984. After only three or four months, my friend decided she wanted out of the partnership, so I bought her share, took over the loans, and I became the sole owner of the business. I sensed that the lab would be successful, and I loved running it.

My full-service medical lab tested patients for drugs, pregnancy, infections, chemistry makeup, and hematology.

The business was off to a good start, but we were barely scraping by in the beginning. We knew we needed an infusion of cash if the business was going to grow. I got approved for another small loan from the US Small Business Administration (SBA), but it wasn't enough to build the business the way I envisioned it.

And when I later applied for a larger loan of about one hundred thousand dollars to expand the business, I was initially rejected.

"I'm sorry," a man at the SBA told me over the phone. "The board voted to turn you down." "Your little business is considered risky," he said.

"The business is small right now, but we're doing so well," I told him. "I don't understand why we would be considered risky."

There was a pause on the other end of the line. "Well," he said, lowering his voice, "a certain woman on the board strongly urged the other board members to vote against you. It is the board's belief that women don't own successful medical labs."

Was he saying I had been rejected, not because the board felt my business model was flawed, but because the lab was run by a woman? And *another woman* on the board had talked the others into voting against me? It felt like a slap in the face.

I was furious, and I was not about to walk away quietly. I called then-congressman Tip O'Neill's office in Washington, DC.

"I'd like to speak with the congressman about the fact that I've been discriminated against," I told one of his aides on the phone.

After laying out the story, I guess they made a flurry of phone calls on my behalf, because later that very day, I received a call from the man with the SBA.

"Chris, I have some good news," he said, mumbling something about a mistake that had been made earlier. "Your loan has been approved." I was relieved that my business would get a fair shot at being successful. But I also felt a sense of satisfaction that I had not allowed the SBA to steamroll me. I was amazed at how quickly a door that had been closed tightly to me was suddenly and miraculously opened thanks to a few phone calls from people in high places.

It was an eye-opener for me, my first glimpse at just how much power the government has.

## Work, Work, Work — That Was My Life

My business continued to grow and thrive — so much so that I had to move the company to larger and larger buildings to house our growing staff and patients. I finally invested in a ten-thousand- square-foot building. At that point, I had about thirty workers on the payroll, including my mother, who helped with billing, and my sister Donna, who was handling the accounting.

The business was doing well, but I was reaching the point of burnout. I was completely immersed in my work, spending at least sixty hours a week at the lab. When I wasn't at the lab, I was thinking about the lab.

"You need to slow down, take time to go out to dinner and relax every once in a while," my then-boyfriend Jim urged. "You're working so hard that you're going to make yourself sick."

I realized that while I had put my head down and worked hard, I had let the years pass me by. I had let my drive for success squeeze out just about every aspect of my personal life. I rarely went out with friends, and I wasn't finding much time for Jim, either.

Work filled the gaps that people had once occupied. All the pain in my life had turned me into a workaholic. It was nice to be in control of my life and not deal with all the pain and emptiness I thought I could forget or outrun.

After running the business for less than five years, it was flourishing. Two separate companies offered to buy me out, and I decided it was time to take a break from the lab and move on to something else.

In 1988, I sold the tiny medical lab that I had started with a mere nine thousand dollars in loans for one and a half million dollars.

I took some time off after selling the medical lab. I started attending mass at a Catholic church more regularly and went on spiritual trips to Medjugorje with my sister-in-law. I realized that God had not been a strong enough presence in my life. I decided that no matter what I did next, God would play a more central role.

What I didn't know then was just how much I would need God to lean on in the years ahead.

## Commitment to Jim

Jim and I had dated for six years, and in that time, our love grew strong and solid. After returning from a spiritual trip, I knew in my heart that I was ready to make the commitment.

"Let's do it," I told him. "I'm ready to start our life together."
In February, 1989, we got married in a small, fairly private civil ceremony, with just a handful of family members. A few months later, we had a big Catholic wedding, celebrating our union with all of our family members and friends. I found the love of my life.

## New Business Venture in 1990

While I was in the process of selling my medical lab, I was toying with the idea of opening a home health care business, but I was approached by two reputable radiologists about opening a diagnostic center, and I had to admit, the business venture sounded intriguing.

In 1990, I agreed to go into business with these doctors and used the proceeds from selling the lab to open a women's diagnostic center. This center would provide ultrasound, mammography, and X-rays. I hired some family members, including two of my sisters.

We had three highly skilled X-ray radiologists with solid reputations; these doctors also worked at a local hospital. I knew that many of the women who walked through the doors of our diagnostic center were facing a true turning point in their lives. Maybe it was a happy time—a pregnant woman eager to see the first ultrasound images of her growing baby. Or maybe it was a time of fear—a woman who had found a lump in her breast and needed our machines to determine whether it was something serious.

I set out to make the diagnostic center welcoming, comforting, and cozy for all of the women who came through our doors. I painted the walls mauve; I hung pretty wallpaper in the dressing rooms; and I put up pictures of smiling mothers with their young children.

And at first, the business thrived. Women heard about the warm atmosphere we had worked hard to create, and little by little, patients who used the hospital for diagnostic services were starting to come my way instead. After all, at my center they had access to the same highly skilled radiologists the hospital employed, yet my place didn't have the cold, sterile, institutional feel of a hospital.

"I like it here," women would tell me. "I feel like I can relax. It doesn't have that hospital smell that makes me nervous."

But our success clearly did not sit well with the newly hired CEO of the nearby hospital, and my radiologists were telling me he might try to buy out my business. At that time, selling my business was the farthest thought from my mind. Still, I accepted an invitation to meet with the CEO at his hospital, because I figured I should hear him out.

"I'm impressed with your diagnostic center," the CEO said as I sat down in his office. "But it looks like you're taking a lot of my business away."

"I think there's enough business for both of us," I said, immediately bristling at his cold tone.

"You are stealing a piece of my revenue," the CEO said, his eyes turning to steel. "I think you should work for me instead."

"Why would I want to work for you when I have my own business?" I asked, incredulous.

"Well, for one thing, if you work for me, I won't have to put you out of business."

His words hung in the air for a moment. I almost couldn't believe what he was saying. *Was this a threat?* I didn't take kindly to threats. I had vowed a long time ago not to let anyone push me around again—ever—especially a man. I had learned to be competitive in a man's world, and I didn't like to lose.

"There's no way you're going to put me out of business," I said angrily as I stood up, ready to storm out of his office. "But if you're going to try, let it begin."

Sure enough, the CEO began putting together fliers filled with a bunch of lies, claiming that I was working for a competing hospital, and he handed out the fliers to doctors who were affiliated with his hospital, urging them not to make any patients' appointments at my center.

I contacted my attorney, who sent a letter to the CEO, threatening to take legal action if he didn't stop disseminating the fliers. This only infuriated the CEO more, and he stepped his efforts up a notch. He went straight to my radiologists and threatened their jobs at the hospital.

"Chris, we have to choose—either the hospital or you," one of the radiologists told me. "If we stay with you, we'll lose our jobs at the hospital."

My heart sank. I knew the radiologists would never choose me over the hospital. And I realized too late that I had only handshake deals with them. They seemed to feel they were free to walk away from my diagnostic center whenever they wanted, without consequence. I watched almost in shock as all three walked out the door. They did so without so much as an apology.

I tried hiring new doctors, but they didn't come with the great reputation these radiologists had; as a result, we were suddenly struggling to bring in patients. Plus, a company that had flirted with buying me out had heard about the fleeing radiologists, and that deal quickly dried up. I was losing money rapidly, and I began telling my employees — including the family members and friends who worked for me — that they should seek other work, because I was afraid I was going down fast.

In 1991, just eighteen months after opening the second business, I was forced to shut it down.

## Mourning the Loss of My Business

I had invested every penny I had earned from the sale of the medical lab into that diagnostic center. Now all of that money had slipped through my fingers.

I wanted to sue the hospital and the radiologists, but my lawyer told me they had "charitable immunity" like all nonprofits did, and that I probably wouldn't get much, if any, money, even if I won. At the time, I didn't care. The hospital had set out to destroy my business, and the doctors had turned their backs on me. It was more about the principle than the money.

The hospital hired a prestigious Boston law firm, and I quickly watched my own legal expenses add up. I tapped into the little bit of savings my husband and I had, and after spending between thirty and forty thousand dollars in legal fees, I was out of money. I was forced to release my attorney.

Coincidentally, a local Boston television station, Channel 5, contacted me around this time to follow up on a previous story they had done on my then-growing business. I quickly seized the opportunity and called the hospital's attorney.

"A TV station wants to do a story about me," I told him. "I'm ready to tell them everything about how the hospital destroyed my successful business."

There was a pause on the other end of the line, and I knew I had him.

"OK," the hospital's attorney said. "What is it going to take?"

The hospital awarded me a hundred thousand dollars.

Although it felt good to make the hospital pay, that money was a drop in the bucket compared to all that I had lost — and all that I still owed. I had signed my name to everything for the business, and the losses included a million-dollar building and medical equipment that cost hundreds of thousands of dollars. Even though financially, I was in a deep hole, I was determined not to file for corporate bankruptcy. I was determined to crawl out of debt.

It meant selling all the computers and medical equipment I could. And when that wasn't enough, I sat quietly by as my own personal belongings were stripped away from me. The IRS auctioned off my new thirty-thousand dollar Porsche for nine thousand dollars; I gave the Mercedes back to the dealer; and the IRS took sixty thousand dollars from my bank account. I even offered to give the IRS some jewelry to settle my debts, but they declined.

For ten years, I had no credit as a result of that disastrous failure. When I tried to apply for an American Express credit card, I was refused, because the IRS had placed a lien against me, claiming that I still owed them two thousand dollars. I thought everything had been resolved with the IRS, but apparently it was not. So for ten years, because my credit was trashed, I used cash or my ATM card to pay for everything.

Even worse — when the business failed, my friends and family members were suddenly out of work, too. My two sisters who had worked for me both ended up financially strapped.
Donna couldn't find another job in Massachusetts and moved to the south, and my sister Carly and her husband lost their home and also moved out of state.

Guilt and regret overwhelmed me, and I found myself replaying over and over, in my mind, what had happened, trying to figure out whether I could have done anything differently to save the business. I felt solely responsible for my sisters' struggles, and it was painful to watch them move away. I wanted so much to help them, but I was in no position to help anyone. It was my first brush in business with complete and total failure, and in the process, I had let so many people down — people I cared about deeply.

I vowed then that if I was ever able to recover anything, if I ever came into any kind of money again, I would take care of them. I felt I owed them.

I felt emotionally abandoned. Family members were moving away, and it was my fault. At the same time, I also noticed that some of my so-called friends suddenly disappeared after the business failed. In particular, two women I thought were close friends, who would often spend the weekend with me and even borrowed my Mercedes to take it for a spin, stopped coming by. Once the business was gone, I would call them and never receive a call back. I never heard from them again. I figured they didn't want to be seen with me anymore, because I had lost everything.

It was tough to lose all that money. But what I learned during that difficult and lonely period was that losing the important people in my life was much harder than losing the money.

Also, after running two businesses, I found myself virtually unemployable. I sent my resume to plenty of companies but was told again and again that I was overqualified for most jobs.

"You've already owned your businesses," interviewers would say. "I'm sure you can never work for someone else again."

I didn't even have the choice of reentering the workforce as a lab tech. When I had sold the medical lab, I had signed an agreement that I wouldn't work at a competing company within twenty-five miles for four years. I didn't know what to do. Several months passed, a year went by and still no work. I felt doomed.

## Life with Jim

Luckily, I had given Jim twenty-five thousand dollars after selling the first business, which he used to buy a small house in the suburbs. He'd purchased the house in his name only. When my business crumbled, we were thankful I hadn't signed onto the mortgage, because we could have lost that, too.

Jim was working as a chemical testing engineer, but his salary was modest, and we were barely making it. Bills piled up, and we couldn't afford more than one car. The emotional and financial stress was straining our marriage. Jim's work life continued as usual; he left for work every morning. Yet my career had come to a screeching halt. I went from being a workaholic to suddenly feeling like I was standing still. I had nowhere to go; there were no appointments to keep.

Later, I did file a lawsuit against the radiologists who abandoned the business, intent on seeking some sort of restitution for the fact that they had reneged on our business arrangement, even though it had only been a verbal arrangement. After all, they were the ones who had initially approached me to start the business, and yet I was the one who ended up financially destroyed when they abandoned me. But I knew that the lawsuit would not be resolved anytime soon—and in the meantime, I was hurting.

Meanwhile, I was getting depressed and having trouble keeping track of time. Even completing the smallest tasks seemed overwhelming. What was the point of showering in the morning if I had nowhere to go that day? I wasn't convinced Jim really understood my distress.

"Why can't you just go and get a job?" he would ask me.

"I'm trying, Jim," I would tell him. "I really am trying, but nothing is coming through."

It sounded so easy — getting a job. Yet I spun my wheels for months. I sent out my resume repeatedly, but nothing happened. And with every rejection, my self-confidence took a hit. I began to wonder why anyone would want to hire me.

I admit that during the heyday of running those two successful businesses, I had gotten a bit cocky. I had started to think I could do no wrong. Now that it was all gone, my ego took a huge hit. I went from wielding all this power to feeling like a victim, and I felt unable to change it.

I had been brave when I started the businesses. Yet, my decision to go up against a big hospital was incredibly naïve. After my business failed, I told myself that I needed to watch myself in the future. It was OK to work hard, but I vowed to steer clear of wrestling with the big guns again. Well, that worked for a little while — until the next time I had to do the right thing.

And I had to wonder: *Would I ever again be able to take the kind of big risks I took in getting those businesses started? Would I ever feel as bold and sure of myself?* During those months I was unemployed, I felt like someone had stolen my boldness roadmap, and I was lost. I had no sense of direction or purpose and no clue how I would brush myself off and move on, either emotionally or financially.

I realized during that long, dark period that I had poured all of my time and energy into one business and then the next, and now that they were gone, I wasn't sure who I was. So many of my physical belongings were gone, but, even worse,

I felt like a huge part of me had been taken away as well. And so I had to ask myself: *What was left? Who am I?*

For fifteen months, in between searching for work, I found myself drawn to the beach, no matter what the weather. I knelt in the sand, tears running down my cheeks, as I closed my eyes and prayed for God's help.

## Finally, a Job

Eventually, my prayers were answered.

In 1993, after more than a year out of work, my cousin found a job with the health insurer, Blue Cross Blue Shield, and she helped get me in for an interview. I almost couldn't believe it when the company hired me. I didn't even care that I was going from owning a multi-million dollar business to getting paid seven dollars an hour. It was a job, and after getting rejected more times than I could count, I was grateful for it.

I was trained in Rockland and started working in Hingham, both suburbs south of Boston. I reviewed medical claims in order to decide which ones met the criteria for payment by Blue Cross. The company did spot checks of my work, and when my reviews were found to be accurate, I was rewarded. I saw my hourly wage climb quickly — it was sixteen dollars an hour within a few months.

Despite making better money, I was irritated with the way the supervisors treated us. The managers monitored every break, including runs to the restroom, to the point where it felt like we were all on the clock every minute of the workday. Having been a manager myself, it bothered me to see employees treated like cattle.

One cold winter day, I was driving my old Chevy to work when it broke down on the expressway. Since the temperature had dipped below zero, I knew I couldn't stay in the unheated car for long and decided to walk toward the next exit, where I figured I could seek some assistance. Sometimes highways offer emergency roadside phones for stranded motorists, but that wasn't an option, and boy was it cold.

Meanwhile, my cousin had grown concerned when I didn't show up for work, so she got in her car to look for me. She never found me, but we both ended up getting back to the office at about the same time. When we tried to explain to our supervisor what had happened, our boss dismissed our story as an excuse.

"Sorry, ladies, but you should have been here," our boss said. "I'm going to have to write both of you up for missing work. Please don't let it happen again."

My cousin and I looked at each other, and I could see in her eyes the same displeasure I felt. It was frustrating, but when you're in that kind of job with that kind of boss, what can you do? What can you say? If you talk back, you'll likely dig yourself into an even worse situation and possibly get fired for mouthing off. I needed that job; I couldn't afford to lose it.

Jim and I were still scraping by at this point and couldn't afford a new car, so after that Chevy died, my husband would drop me off at a gas station every morning to meet up with my cousin, and she would drive me to work.

## Boxes and Boxes of Unprocessed Claims

For several months, I plugged away at my job, and then something strange happened: a health care provider contacted me.

"I am getting fed up," the doctor said. "I have been waiting for Blue Cross to pay my office's claims for a very long time. In fact, I have waited so long that I might even have to shut my business down if I don't get my money sometime soon. You have to realize how much this is hurting me."

"I'm sorry to hear that, sir. I'm not sure what's going on," I said. "But I will look into it and get back to you. I promise."

I didn't really know what he was talking about. I figured at first that there must have been some mistake, and the office had somehow missed a payment. But when I tried to search for his claims, I had trouble finding any record of them.

I started asking around, and a fellow worker explained nonchalantly, "Oh yeah, we have '90ed' those claims," he said. "Those claims are on hold. We'll get to them eventually."

In order to receive Medicare payments from the government, Blue Cross had to process a claim within a certain number of days, but because the company was short on staff, employees had trouble meeting those deadlines. So employees were told to enter code 90 into the computer system, which was an internal code that made it appear as if the claim had been processed. By doing so, Blue Cross would get its money from the government. Some of the claims that were well over forty-five days old were deleted from the system or were given false dates, and others were hidden in drawers of empty desks.

Although Blue Cross was getting reimbursed, it was not processing those code 90 claims and therefore was not paying the doctors in a timely manner. The claims were in limbo. I thought about that poor doctor who was waiting on thousands of dollars in unpaid bills. I had been one of those health care providers at one time, and I believed the doctor who told me that his small practice depended on those payments, and that without them, he would have to shut down. I knew there had to be many other doctors just like him who were also waiting for payments.

I understood worrying about paying bills. It was still a sensitive topic and stressor for Jim and me. Maybe that's what struck a nerve with me. In any event, I was intent on helping this doctor.

"Where are the 90ed claims kept?" I asked a coworker. I tried to keep my voice casual, neutral. I have always felt like an open book, that my face always betrayed my feelings, whether I wanted it to or not. But I tried to be careful. I didn't want anyone to know how much this practice of tossing aside claims bugged me.

"Oh, we put those 90ed claims in a storage room," my colleague said.

And sure enough, I discovered the claims were thrown into boxes and placed in an adjacent storage room. I stood in the doorway of that storage room astounded, my mouth gaping, as I took in the sight of box after box after box, piled several feet high. When I thought about the fact that each claim was only one thin piece of paper, I had to wonder how many thousands or even millions of claims were getting shoved aside. Would they ever be processed?

"There are a lot of claims in that storage room," I said to the coworker. "How long have they been sitting there?"

"Oh, it depends," the coworker said. "Some of them haven't been in there that long, maybe a few weeks or months. But some of them have probably been in there for a year or longer."

## Internal Audit

A year? The claims had been sitting there, gathering dust, for that long? When would anyone ever get around to processing them? When would the doctors ever receive the money we owed them?

"Well, what will happen to them?" I asked. "Will they ever get paid?"

My coworker shrugged, seemingly unconcerned. "I guess so — when we can get it done." Coincidentally, around this same time, members of an accounting firm were combing through the office, because Blue Cross was undergoing an internal audit. I became friendly with a member of the accounting team, and I took the woman aside.

"Something really bad is going on here," I said, keeping my voice low. I pointed out the boxes of 90ed claims. "Are you able to do something about it?"

That auditor seemed concerned as her eyes took in the stacked boxes. So I waited, wondering whether the company would be called to act on all those claims. But several weeks passed, and nothing happened.

So I called the vice president of Blue Cross and pointed out the problem. Maybe the higher-ups didn't know what was going on.

"What they're doing is wrong," I said.

"I promise I'm going to look into it, Chris," the vice president said. "Thank you for giving me this information regarding the claims in Medical Review."

Sure, he had expressed some concern on the phone, yet even more weeks passed, and still nothing happened. I kept an eye on the storage room, and no one ever went in there — except to dump more 90ed claims. The boxes didn't move.

I was getting increasingly impatient with the lack of response. So I began writing letters about it. I wrote to congressmen and to then- President Bill Clinton and his wife Hillary. The White House responded, saying I should contact the US Attorney General's Office. I called my attorney, who suggested we file what is known as a qui tam lawsuit — a whistleblower complaint — on behalf of the federal government against Blue Cross.

If the government found that the company had committed fraud and fined the company for its wrongdoing, my attorney explained that I would stand to be awarded a portion of that fine just for turning in the company.

"I'm going to file a complaint," I told a few coworkers I trusted. "Do you want to go in on this with me? We could file a complaint and pursue a case together."

But I watched as, time and time again, a look of fear came over my coworkers' eyes at the mere mention of a complaint. They seemed uncomfortable even talking about it, and they all declined to get involved.

"I could never do that," one coworker told me. "I would be too afraid I might lose my job."

As it turns out, a former employee who had gotten fired from Blue Cross had gone to the government before I did. My attorney talked to that woman's attorney in an effort to get me involved in the case, but the manager did not want to let me in. According to the whistleblower rules, the first to file a whistleblower complaint is the only one capable of receiving an award.

In September 1994, Blue Cross Blue Shield of Massachusetts was indeed forced to pay $2.75 million to settle allegations that the company submitted false Medicare reports in processing Medicare claims for Massachusetts, Maine, New Hampshire, and Vermont.

My attorney felt badly that my complaint had come in later than the other one and that I wouldn't receive a portion of those fines. At the time, I didn't really understand how a qui tam complaint worked, and to be honest, I didn't really care about any of the legalities involved, so I didn't ask many questions.

Getting shut out of the whistleblower award didn't bother me much. Although the money would have been nice, I wasn't really after that. I just wanted Blue Cross to stop 90ing claims and to start paying its health care providers. It was satisfaction enough to know that the company's inappropriate practices had been exposed and that the company was punished for its illegal activities.

In the midst of the company's punishment, I was abruptly fired. I imagine the vice president I had called probably figured out that I was one of the people who had complained to the government.

As I came into work one day, my manager walked quickly to my desk with a deep frown on her face, and I knew something was up.

"You're going to need to pack up your belongings and leave the office right away," she said. "You're being fired."

I stared at her, my heart pounding. I guess I should have known this was a possibility, but I still felt somehow unprepared. I couldn't believe they could get away with letting me go.

"Why am I being fired?" I asked, my voice shaking.

"I can't get into that with you right now, Chris," my manager answered coldly. "You're going to need to start packing up now."

Just then, two security guards appeared at my desk and waited. There was no point in trying to talk about it or fight it. I just needed to go.

As I began putting picture frames, coffee cups, and other personal items into a box, I felt the eyes of my coworkers on me. Some of them knew that I had filed a complaint against the company. I wanted to say good-bye to them, but when I opened my mouth to speak to a coworker who was sitting nearby, my manager stopped me.

"Sorry, Chris, but you're not allowed to speak to the other workers right now," she said. "It's time to go."

As the security guards escorted me out of the building, I felt a strange mixture of embarrassment and pride. It was scary and upsetting to get fired, yet I knew I had done the right thing by exposing the truth, and if I had to lose my job as a result of reporting the company, so be it. Besides, in a way it was a relief to leave a company that wasn't treating me or any of its other workers well.

I wondered if any of my coworkers would reach out to me later, to tell me they thought what the company had done was wrong. But no one—not a soul except the cousin I had worked with—bothered to call me. And I wasn't about to call them. I decided to put the whole awful experience behind me. *I have been through worse, haven't I?* I thought.

It took me several months to find another job, this time as an office manager for a pediatrician in Plymouth. I had been working there for only six months when my world was turned upside down. My mother—the family member I had always relied on most for love and support—suddenly died.

## The Loss of My Mother

My mother was a lifelong New Englander—a little tough on the outside, but incredibly soft on the inside. She wasn't overly affectionate or touchy-feely in the way many mothers are. Yet, I always felt completely secure in my mother's love. She provided a comforting cloak of protection that I nuzzled repeatedly as a child. My siblings may have had a different view of her; I believe some of them saw her as emotionally detached.

And maybe they did see that side of her more than I did. Looking back, I have to wonder if my mother reserved a soft spot in her heart especially for me—maybe she sensed I was the one who needed it most. Mother's Day was approaching, and after having faced the loss of my dad and others I have loved over the years, I knew how difficult the upcoming holidays would be. March 19 would stay in my mind for the rest of my life; that was the day my mom died. Within four hours of arriving at the emergency room, she was gone. The doctors did not know what killed her. The most important person in my life was no longer with me. The pain was so bad that a part of my heart died with her. I will always miss her; she taught me to love unconditionally.

If only I'd had sufficient time to recover from one epic loss before being tested again.

## The Proverbial Calm before the Storm

New Englanders understand how quickly the weather can change some days, especially when transitioning from one season to another. The day can begin with ninety-degree heat and end with snow. I looked ahead and worried about finding a job, paying the bills, and starting a family—basically getting my life back on track, but Jim and I could never have imagined the many challenges, the many storms, we'd experience and survive in a relatively short period of time.

Sometimes we just couldn't catch a break. I've heard people say that difficult events come in threes. Superstition or not, it seemed to be true for us. Every time we got hit hard emotionally or financially, there was another storm brewing right around the corner—like a spectacular firestorm with thunder and lightning colliding and crashing right over our heads.

# Chapter Three: Joining the Company

## Consultant Job at the Company

Not long after my mother's death in 1995, I answered a newspaper ad for a job as a consultant at a giant Swiss biopharmaceutical company with US headquarters in Massachusetts
.

*This woman must wonder what in the world brought me to this company,* I thought as I sat nervously in the interview. I really wanted and needed the job.

During my interview, I barely breathed while the woman from Human Resources reviewed my resume. I pondered what she thought about my scattered work experience; I imagined that I must have seemed almost suspicious on paper. After all, I had owned two medical businesses that had been so successful.

I had lived the high life for a while, but all of those cards had come crashing down when the second business failed, and all of the money and pretty things — fancy jewelry, sports cars, and pricey furniture — had gone with it.

I had been left with next to nothing but my will to survive and my desire to keep on working.

I was thrilled when I later received official word that they decided to hire me as a consultant; this was good timing for me. The loss of my mother had made me long for more meaningful work.

And so my journey began with my new job. I would learn later how a giant biopharmaceutical company does business.

## Learning about AIDS Patients and Serostim

In May, 1995, right around Mother's Day, I was sitting in an interview with Janet, a product manager. Less than two months after joining the company, I had not only been hired on as a permanent employee but was now being considered for a job in reimbursement—making sure doctors and patients were reimbursed by insurance companies for the cost of a drug that helped AIDS patients.

AIDS is a cruel, degenerative disease that takes lives slowly, often painfully. The disease literally attacks patients' insides, shrinks their organs, and, little by little, steals their lives away. Many AIDS patients suffer from wasting syndrome, the loss of lean body mass. If left untreated, wasting can cause death.

The company had created a prescription drug, Serostim, a synthetic growth hormone that helped maintain muscle and organ tissue. It built up a person's body mass and slowed down the wasting away of organs.

I could see that Janet was all fired up about this drug, thrilled that it was helping people.

"We feel strongly that this drug is powerful and can make a big difference in the lives of AIDS patients," Janet said. "We believe it can prolong people's lives."

I nodded, impressed, and felt suddenly eager to land this job. I liked the idea of getting involved in pushing insurance companies to pay for this effective drug.

"We need someone who can be assertive, someone who will fight to make sure patients get the drug they really need," Janet said. "It might involve getting firm with insurance companies, really doing your best to talk them into paying for this drug, because it's expensive. Do you think you might be assertive enough to handle this kind of position?" Janet asked.

"Yes," I said confidently. "I know I can do that."

"Do you have any experience to back that up?" she asked.

"Well," I said, "actually I did fight for the right thing in one of my previous jobs."

I laid out what had happened at Blue Cross Blue Shield. I told her about the boxes of 90ed claims I had found, and I told her I had reported Blue Cross for allegedly defrauding the government.

"I turned them in, because I wanted to fight for the health care providers who deserved to get reimbursed," I said. "What the company was doing was wrong. I tried to tell the vice president about it, but when he didn't do anything, I thought I had to report them to the government. I felt strongly that this was a situation that had to be made right."

I had Janet's attention now. She was sitting forward in her seat, listening intently and nodding her head.

"You did that?" she asked.

"Yes, and it ended up costing me my job at Blue Cross," I said.

At the time, I didn't think about the fact that a pharmaceutical company might not value this kind of action. All drug companies had to remain constantly vigilant, mindful of government regulations, because if the government started snooping around, it was always bad news.

In my mind, I was telling the truth about my experience, and I wasn't ashamed. I wanted Janet to know that I would be a true advocate for suffering patients.

And I could see from the look on her face that she was impressed.

"Wow," she said. "I have to say, that must have taken a lot of guts. And you know, that's exactly the type of employee we want— someone who will fight for our patients."

I knew I had the job then, and a wave of excitement ran through me. Helping seriously ill people get a drug they needed sounded like work I would find personally fulfilling. I felt like I could make a difference in this job, that my mother would walk through it with me and that, ultimately, I would make her and my dad proud.

During that job interview, I was impressed by Janet's intentions and intoxicated by her energy and enthusiasm for this life-saving drug.

Ironically, Janet was one of the employees who would later be taken down in the scandal, indicted for allegedly offering bribes to doctors. I believe that the day of that interview, her heart had been in the right place and she was working on behalf of the patients.

But she moved up the corporate ladder quickly, and the higher you went, the more the money flowed: trips, kickbacks, and salary hikes. Eventually, I believe she got caught up in a whirlwind of greed along with many others.

## Serostim for AIDS Patients

Patients called me when they needed help getting their insurance companies to pay for the drug. Some of the patients were desperate to continue with the prescription, as they raved about its effectiveness.

"Serostim is amazing," patients would tell me. "The drug makes me feel great. I really want to keep taking it, and I need your help to get my insurance company to approve coverage."

Patients even said that they believed the drug was helping them live longer—that was all I needed to know to feel passionate about my work. Many patients wanted to continue using Serostim but were having trouble getting reimbursed, because insurance companies viewed it as an experimental drug.

And in essence, it *was* an experimental drug at that time. The Federal Drug Administration (FDA) had put the medication on a fast track for testing and approval and allowed its use on the market for investigational purposes in 1996, all because the drug was used to treat a life-threatening disease. But the FDA had withheld its full seal of approval, noting that further clinical trials needed to be conducted.

That lack of full approval ended up looking like a big red flag to insurance companies, leading many to quickly reject all Serostim claims.

I was relentless on the phone with insurance companies, fighting to get them to reimburse doctors and patients for a drug that was saving people's lives. I called medical directors and talked to them about what I was hearing from patients— that the drug worked better than anything else on the market.

I sensed that the insurance companies knew I believed in this drug, and it seemed to help open their wallets.

"Normally we wouldn't reimburse for a drug like this, but under the circumstances, if it is saving people's lives, we will pay," company reps would tell me.

## Wanting a Family

During this time, my husband and I were on a life-changing journey: we had decided to adopt a child.
We had both always wanted to have children. Years earlier, I had gotten pregnant but didn't know it, because I was still getting my period. At the same time, I sought medical treatment for an enlarged spleen, and I was given drugs that were considered toxic to a fetus—only to find out shortly afterward that I was four months pregnant. Doctors told me the drugs I had taken would be extremely harmful to the developing fetus and urged me to end the pregnancy.

I am a devout Catholic. I don't believe in abortion. And I wanted so much to have a child, but I was filled with fear that the medication I had taken had inadvertently harmed the baby inside me. I had watched as my younger sister Donna had given birth to a daughter who had multiple deformities— a little girl who died at only nine months old.

I saw how much that experience had crushed my sister, and I was afraid if I had the baby, I would be going down the same heart- wrenching path. I was torn, so I consulted with some Catholic doctors, all of whom opposed abortion, but under the circumstances, they all advised me that I should move ahead with the procedure.

So at the doctors' urging, I agreed to have a therapeutic abortion. I skipped out on one of the appointments, still unsure and fearful I would be filled with regret. But I did keep the next one — and I cried long and hard over the loss of my child. I still feel the loss; it will haunt me forever that I had listened to Doctors instead of my heart.

A few months later, when my husband and I tried to conceive another child, we found we were unable to do so — even with the help of fertility drugs. Not long after that, we decided we would open our home to a foster child.

We hadn't gotten that far down the road of taking courses and preparing for an adoption through the state's foster care system when we suddenly got a phone call that a five-year-old girl needed a home on an emergency basis. Jim and I were excited, and my bosses even threw me a big baby shower at work, giving me stuffed animals and clothes for the child.

My bosses were so supportive, even telling me I could take time off if I needed it. I liked being part of a company that cared about its people. Loyalty means a lot to me, and during those early days at work, I really loved my job. I felt like I was giving back and doing well.

The girl came to us through a social services adoption agency in Quincy, but the social workers had given us very little information about her. We later found out that Brenda our new addition had been physically and sexually abused by family members from a very early age while in the Foster Care system. It didn't take long after her arrival in our Marshfield home for the girl to start acting out.

Day care workers told us she would lay on top of other children, tell them to take their clothes off, and touch them. The girl also had tremendous rage and would blow up on us without warning — and each time she did so, it triggered an unsettling sense of anger in me as well.

At first we tried to work with her, to help her and provide a comforting home for her in hopes that with therapy, she would adjust. But I saw the empty, bitter look in her eyes, and I decided that no matter what we did for her, she might never be whole.

As I watched her struggle with a past that she couldn't prevent from haunting her, I realized that I would never be able to help her — and that was because I needed help myself to deal with some things that had happened to me, things I had brushed aside for many years.

This little girl was bringing all of it to the surface.

Jim and I called the state's Department of Social Services, discussed what was going on, and we all decided that we were not equipped to deal with Brenda's problems. Social workers advised us to bring her to a hospital where she would be placed in special housing with other children who had endured abuse. We hugged her, explained that we were leaving her with people who would care for her, and we struggled to keep our composure as we said our good-byes.

She looked at us with eyes filled with confusion, and our hearts felt like they were breaking. Life would never be the same, not a day goes by that I do not think of her and all the harm that had been done to this poor child.

Yes, she was no longer in our home, which may sound like a problem solved; but for us, it wasn't that simple. Jim and I had fallen in love with this little girl. We thought she was a gift from God—a gift from my mother, as well—and to lose her felt like a huge failure on our part. Even worse, my husband said he couldn't think about ever adopting a child again. He couldn't bear to fall for another child and take the risk that it might not work out.

Not only did I lose the little girl I had grown attached to, I also lost my dream of having a family. It was killing me inside. I felt that I had failed my mother and God just one more time. I would never be able to recover from this pain.

Jim and I decided to take action against the adoption agency that had placed the girl in our home. They should have told us about her abusive past—if they had, we never would have started this process with her, and because we knew we would never be able to handle a child with such severe problems. We could have spared her—and ourselves—from the false hope that the three of us would become a family. So Jim and I filed a complaint against the adoption agency, and the state later shut the place down.

## Free-Falling into an Emotional Hole

I began to spiral into despair. I went to church over and over, the place where I usually found comfort and peace, searching for a way to feel better. But no matter how often I went, I couldn't find my way out of the emotional hole I felt myself falling into. I looked at myself in the mirror—my unsmiling face, my dark, dead eyes—and I saw no light. All I could see was loss: the loss of my unborn child, the loss of my mother, the loss of the little girl, and the loss of who I was. I could see my own disappointment; I had failed again.

One day, as I was driving home from work, I fantasized about veering off the road and hitting a tree. *What would it matter?* I thought. *Life didn't seem worth living anymore.*

*I knew that I needed help, that if I did not get help soon I might fall further into depression and despair.*

My husband was dealing with his own grief over losing the child— so much so that I don't think he was truly aware of just how deeply I was suffering. However, one important person in my life did notice: my brother-in-law Ben. Shortly before the adoption, Ben, my sister Lisa's husband, had been out of work for a while, and I had helped him get an interview at the company. He had gotten the job. We worked side by side, and Ben could see that I was having trouble concentrating at work and seemed to be falling into a depression. He reached out to me.

"Hey, I know you're going through a tough time," he said to me quietly. "I am here to listen whenever you want to talk."

I was pretty sure he was also reporting back to my sister Lisa that I wasn't doing well, because she was calling me, too. His concern meant a lot to me. I was grateful for his attempts at throwing me a lifeline, and yet I was unable to reach for it. I had no energy to accept any offers for help.

In the spring, I went to church one day and prayed like I had never prayed before, desperate to feel a sense of inner peace. Church was always the place that could make me feel good again, but on that day, I could not feel God's comforting presence. I felt as if God were rejecting me. I felt in my heart that he had given me a second chance to redeem myself after my abortion by allowing us to adopt the little girl, and I had let him down. I had failed. The malaise I had been feeling burst through that day into a flood of tears that I couldn't stop.

I realized that I could not pull myself out of my own depression and needed help — serious help.

I was supposed to head down to North Carolina to visit my sister Donna, but I looked at my husband through wet and weary eyes and said, "I'm not happy. I just want to sleep and stay asleep."

I knew that I had to take drastic action right then, or I might never recover. "I need you to take me to a psychiatric hospital. I need help," I said.

Jim looked surprised and a little scared. "Are you sure you need to do that?" he asked, clearly worried that I wasn't thinking things through.

"Yes, I need to go, and I need to go right away," I insisted.

Later that day, after getting my primary care doctor to approve a residential stay at a psychiatric hospital in my area, Jim drove me there as I stared silently out the window. I had left home in such haste that I had not even packed a bag.

When we arrived at the hospital, the staff asked me to empty my pockets, and they searched my purse.

I was placed in a room with a young girl who had tried to kill herself. Her boyfriend had left her, and she had taken an overdose of pills. My roommate seemed out of it, lost in her own troubles, so I left her alone. I started to realize what I had done by signing myself in to the hospital; I could not leave until the doctors gave me the OK.

I made my way to the TV room, and a male patient approached me. "What are you doing here?" he asked.

"I'm here because I need to deal with some issues from my past," I told him.

"So am I," the man said, then added: "I always end up at the playground. Something always attracts me to little kids."

I knew then that this man was confessing that he was a sexual predator. I froze, unable to speak as I felt intense anger coursing through me.

I was trying to take all of this in and couldn't help but think, of all the people in this place, one of the first people I had to talk to was a pedophile? Are you kidding me? I felt a strong rage right then and there. I wanted to kill the guy for what he had done to other children—children just like the little girl I had tried to adopt … and children just like me. I spoke to the nurse, and I never saw the man again. When I asked, they told me they had sent him away.

## Reliving My Past

All at once, it hit me hard—everything that I have been through. I had pushed it all aside for so many years and had told myself that I was OK. But suddenly it was all coming to the surface at once, and I couldn't stop any of it.

For the first two days in the hospital, I paced my room, nibbled at the food and wandered somewhat aimlessly through the rooms.

I had checked myself in to the psychiatric hospital on a Saturday, and it took two days before I was able to see any doctors. On Monday, I began attending group therapy sessions. I sat in a circle with other patients, and at first I held back and quietly listened to other people's stories.

One woman recounted how she was repeatedly raped by a priest. Another woman, an anorexic, was wasting away to nothing, and yet when she was asked to draw a picture of herself, she drew herself as huge and said she felt she didn't have enough paper to draw how big she truly was — one piece of paper was not large enough. Another woman who was suicidal had had shock therapy treatment, and I could see the difference in her when she returned from her treatment: her face was blank, her memory shot.

I was amazed at the accomplishments of some of the patients. One was an obstetrician whose life was a mess; another was a lawyer who had been mugged and beaten and had lost part of her memory as a result.

The lawyer's parents came to visit her one day, and they were very well-to-do, and were on their way to a charitable function. They were chatting away casually around their daughter. They seemed almost too busy to bother with her and were ready to rush off within minutes of arriving. The lawyer got very upset after her parents left, and the staff worried that she was suicidal, so they took her to the lockdown area, where patients are locked in a bare room. A lot of people ended up in those rooms. At some point, I realized that if I didn't open up and share the stories of the abuse I had endured, I would end up as lost and hopeless as that lawyer.

So I started talking. And once I started, it all came flooding out in big waves. All the ways I had been done wrong — both as a child and as an adult.

## Waiting for Daylight

It felt strange at first to talk about those things — horrific things that I had worked so hard to push down and forget.
I had always kept those things inside, ugly secrets that I never

dared to share with loved ones or friends. I kept those things hidden, because there was a part of me that wondered if people would judge me by some of my worst moments.

Maybe that's because, in a way, I had always judged myself.

But there in the hospital, with patients who were suffering from some deep wounds of their own, I felt safe enough to let it out and work through it.

It started when I was young. I slept over someone's house on the living room sofa. In the middle of the night while I was sleeping, a man slipped his hand inside my underpants and began touching me. I was sleepy at first and didn't really understand what was happening. I could smell alcohol on his breath. I remember saying, "No, don't."

It felt uncomfortable, wrong. He didn't stop right away, and I didn't know what to do. I was afraid to move, afraid to breathe. I closed my eyes and tried to keep my fear in check by focusing on the ticking of the clock in the kitchen. He was probably with me for only a short time, but it felt like forever.

Finally, he got up and left without a word. After he was gone, I felt frozen on the sofa, too scared to move or sleep, and I waited hour after hour for daylight to come. I couldn't wait for sunrise, because I felt that once the sun came up, I would feel safe. I longed to see the kitchen bright and sunny again; because I felt then I would know that the man wouldn't be back, that it was all over.

Weeks later, I went with other relatives to an amusement park north of Boston. I must have been acting a little quiet and strange, because a relative asked me what was wrong when the two of us were alone. Without thinking, I blurted out what had happened.

This relative shot me a look, her eyes dark and cold.

"No, that did not happen," she hissed. "You're making it up. How could you do that? You're evil."

I sat and stared at her, horrified. She didn't believe me. It had never occurred to me that she might accuse me of lying. I clammed up the rest of the day and decided it was best to push down what had happened and never tell another soul. Surely, if this relative didn't believe me, no one else would either.

When I was dropped off at home later that day, I ran into my house and, without warning, the tears came. Before I knew it, I was sobbing hysterically in my room. My mother came in and began asking questions.

"What's wrong?" she wanted to know. But I refused to tell her. I was so afraid my mother wouldn't believe me, and I couldn't bear that. Besides, I figured what had happened must have been my fault somehow. Why else would that relative have reacted so angrily? *Maybe I really was evil*, I thought.

My mother tried for a while to get me to talk, but when it was clear that I wouldn't, she backed off. But she did tell me: "You never have to go to that house again," and she kept her word. Shortly before my mother died, I shared the details of that incident. It was clear from our conversation that my mother had figured out what had happened back then and that she was determined to protect me from future harm by keeping me away from my relative.

I pushed the incident down for many years and tried hard not to think about it. But looking back, I realized it had clearly affected me. As a young girl, I suddenly became wary of men. I didn't want to be touched or hugged for many years afterward. Unfortunately, that would not be the last time a man harmed me.

## A Night of Revelry Gone Wrong

When I was eighteen and still living at home with my parents, I took a trip into Boston on New Year's Eve with some cousins and a friend — all girls. After drinking a little beer during the car ride into the city, we parked our car and started walking around without any real plan or destination; we were just excited to be on our own, looking to drink and find some fun.

While we were walking around downtown Boston, a van stopped, and a guy inside shouted, "Hey, do you girls want to party with us?"

We were young and naïve and we eagerly jumped into the van and accepted paper cups of beer from the three guys, two white and one black. The men appeared to be in their mid-twenties and had already begun to party. While we sat and chatted, I sipped my beer. I hadn't had that much to drink, but I started feeling lightheaded and a little sick to my stomach. I later figured out that my drink had been spiked with a drug. I was feeling out of it, but I had the vague awareness that my friends were making plans. "We're going to leave and get the car and come back for you, Chris," my cousin told me.

I wanted to go with them, but I felt incredibly sluggish, and my mind wouldn't will my body to move. I opened my mouth to speak, to tell them to wait for me, but I was too out of it, unable to form the words. Before I knew it, the other girls had piled out of the van, leaving me all alone with three men.

And as soon as my friends were gone, the van suddenly took off.

As the drug took over, I found myself in a dreamlike state, believing I was in California — a place I had always wanted to visit — and I briefly drifted off to sleep.

Shortly afterwards I awoke, still in a fog, just as one of the men was ripping off my pants. My mind was telling me to fight, to protect myself, but the drug made me feel weak, powerless. I couldn't move my arms or my legs. As the man raped me, the pain ripped through me, but all I could do was cry and scream over and over, "No, no! It hurts, it hurts! I'm a virgin!" I drifted in and out of consciousness for a while, unsure whether I was being raped by one man or three, until I finally passed out for real.

The next thing I knew, I woke up alone, having been dumped along the side of the road. My pants and T-shirt were ripped, but I pulled my long navy pea coat around me so no one could see my torn clothes. Unsure of where I was and still feeling out of it, I got to my feet and started walking aimlessly across a bridge, staring at a blinking CITGO gas sign and telling myself over and over, "I've got to get home."

It was cold, and I was shivering, but I also felt numb. It was dark, and I had no idea what time it was. I looked around, hoping to spot a street or a landmark I recognized, but everything seemed out of focus, and I knew I was lost.

New Year's revelers were laughing and bustling by, and I was crying as I stopped a few strangers to ask, "Where am I?" and "Can you help me get home?" But people shrugged me off and kept walking, probably assuming I was just drunk like most everyone else that night.

I kept walking, unsure where I was heading, until a guy wearing a fireman's hat pulled up in a car along the sidewalk and asked me if I needed a ride. Desperate, I got into the car.

"Yes," I said. "I need to get back to my friends and family."

I asked the guy to take me to my aunt's home, and somehow I managed to direct him to my aunt's house in Boston. Looking back, it's amazing that I knew how to find it, because I didn't know my way around the area. God must have been with me.

The guy followed my directions, but he was acting a little weird and was starting to make me feel uncomfortable.

"Go tell them you're OK, then come back and party with me," he told me as he stopped in front of my aunt's house. By this point, it was starting to get light out. My cousins had returned home without me, and my family members were wondering about my whereabouts, so my aunt was relieved to see me coming through the door. She peeked out the window at the guy waiting in the car below, and the guy took off.

My aunt never said anything to me, or at least I don't remember her saying anything other than she was glad I was home and safe. She knew from the glazed look in my eyes that something bad had happened to me.

I don't remember much after reaching my aunt's house, but she never asked me where I had been, what had happened, or even why I had been alone. She just looked at me and peeked out the window again to ensure the car below had left and knew my life had been changed for the worse, forever.

"I have to lie down. I don't feel well," I said to my aunt. I wasn't lying—the drugs and the horrific events that had taken place earlier that night made me feel just awful, physically as well as emotionally. I slept for a little while, then ate some cereal and took a long bus ride home to the suburbs that afternoon. I kept my coat on the entire time I was at my aunt's thinking she would just think I was cold—it was the winter after all.

I still remember the pained look in my aunt's eyes when I walked in and out of her house that day. Her funny, wise-cracking, salty language was very much subdued. She let me leave and uncharacteristically didn't hug or kiss me when I entered or when I left her home. And that was just fine with me. We barely looked each other in the eye, but I know she felt my pain.

"Where were you?" my dad asked as I came through the door, knowing that my cousins had returned home much earlier.

"They kind of left me," I said vaguely. "I stayed over mom's sister's house for the night and then took the bus home," I added and tried to ensure I sounded confident and that my coat stayed closed.

"You can never go out with them again," my dad said sternly.

"OK," I mumbled quietly to my dad. That sounded good to me and would be an excuse for not hanging out with those cousins again.

I went to my room and took off my coat — and just then, my mother came into the room and saw my ripped clothing.

"You have to get out of those clothes," she said, and she quietly started running a bath for me. She steered me into the bathroom, helped me into the tub, and began to clean my body. Her eyes scanned the bruises that ran up and down my legs.

"They must have..." my mother started, her voice catching, but I panicked at the thought of her knowing I had been raped. I didn't want to believe that it had happened.

"No, they didn't," I said quickly, then tried to assure her: "I think I'm still a virgin."

After all, not only had I never slept with a man, but I had never had a boyfriend, had never had any intimate moments with guys beyond a couple of innocent kisses.

Even in the comfort of my mother's presence, I felt humiliated, ashamed and afraid that I had somehow lost the most important thing to me — my virginity. I didn't want my parents to know, because I was afraid they would make me feel it was my fault. And I wanted to pretend, even in my own mind, that maybe I still was a virgin. I couldn't bear the thought that a complete stranger had taken that away from me against my will.

"If your dad finds out, he's going to go find those guys," my mother said.

I shivered at the thought of my dad searching for the men. That would make a bad situation so much worse. "Please don't tell him. I don't even know who they are," I said, kicking myself inside for being so naïve and stupid. *We shouldn't have been drinking,* I thought. *We never should have agreed to get into that van with a group of strange men.*

Not long afterward, I went to the doctor. My mom offered to go with me, but I told her I wanted to go by myself, because I still didn't want her to find out, I was no longer a virgin. Years later, I told my mother the truth about that night, and she said she had already assumed what had happened and had informed my dad, who cried upon hearing the news.

After the rape, I tried to push the incident out of my mind, as if it had never happened. I felt that I had survived it, and I was lucky I hadn't gotten pregnant or caught any diseases. I didn't want to talk about it with anyone. I wanted to totally forget it had ever happened, put it into some closed compartment in my mind where I wouldn't have to deal with it.

I would be haunted by that fateful night, even though, for many years, I brushed it aside, thinking it was no big deal. I was OK and I had moved past the trauma. And nobody wanted to talk about it, so I just buried it along with the good memories and the difficult memories, thinking it would remain buried forever.

Try as I might to forget it, though, the gang rape that fateful New Year's Eve stayed with me. I never wanted to go into Boston. I avoided talking to the cousins and friend I had been with that night, because I didn't want them to remind me of the rape. I dreaded New Year's Eve every year and avoided celebrating.

And when I saw a van pass me by on the street, I would panic inside; worried it might be the same men who had attacked me that night. The emotional scars were clearly there, and while I was in the psychiatric hospital, I finally confronted the feelings I had about that awful incident, because I knew it was the only way I would ever completely move past it.

## Emerging from Darkness

But even with Jim as my rock, I realized while I was in the hospital that I would not be able to move on emotionally until I learned to deal with the wrongs I had endured earlier in life.

At the hospital, surrounded by so many lost souls, I began to open up and share stories about the abuse I had endured as a child at the hands of a relative, about the strangers who raped me as a teenager, and about the double loss of my first marriage and my dad. I talked about the angry little girl who had come into my home and heart and then had to leave — the final loss that had brought all the other losses to the surface.

"I came here because I couldn't find God," I confessed during a group meeting after I had been in the hospital a few days. "I couldn't feel **God's** presence anymore, and that scared me."

A young man shot back angrily, "There is no God!" I was taken aback.

Usually when I look into people's eyes, I see light in them — life. I looked into his eyes, and there was total darkness. I looked around at other people's eyes, and I saw more darkness. Sadness and pain were all around me. These people were victims, and they would always be victims. I was afraid of becoming like them. I was afraid I would remain stuck in this place, where people lived in the hell within their own minds.

During my time in the hospital, I had four visitors: my husband, Jim, who brought clothes from home and words of encouragement; and a brother, who told me I had a "bad case of the sads." Later, two nuns came by to visit: one who provided comfort with her words and another who told me, "Satan has put you in here." That nun made me feel worse. It reminded me of praying once and hearing a nun say,

"We have to pray harder because evil is coming," and that made me stop cold in my tracks, because I had thought, "Oh no, I am the one who is evil." Just the word "evil" dredged up the awful memory of my relative calling me an evil child after I had revealed that I had been fondled.

I have no doubt Satan exists. I believe people can be overcome by evil. But I didn't believe what the nun told me, that I was in the hospital because of Satan. And I abruptly stopped talking to that nun. I would never give anyone that power over me except God. I still believe that has all people have good inside them, because God made each one of us, and his light can endure all darkness.

Maybe I had never let go of the notion that perhaps I was somehow partly to blame for the bad things that had happened to me.

Certain events had stuck with me since my childhood, events and words that had hurt me. Being told I wasn't physically attractive enough by my family and my ex- husband stuck with me, as did being told by an aunt and now a nun, that I was evil. I just wanted to feel loved and accepted for who I was.

## Dealing with All the Pain

One day when my husband visited, the hospital told him it was OK for him to take me out for the day. We went to a mall, and I looked at Jim with heavy eyes, feeling the weight of my own sadness. I didn't want to have to worry about being well for anyone else. I wanted to crawl inside my own shell and stay safe inside a padded cell.

"I don't think I want to be married anymore," I told him. "I want to be left alone."

"No," he said firmly. "I'm not going to let you go. Do you understand that?"

With tears in my eyes and a lump in my throat, I nodded. "OK" I said meekly. It would take me a while before I fully appreciated that Jim would remain at my side—no matter what—and it would take me even longer before I realized how much I wanted and needed him there. I was relieved that he was willing to hold me up emotionally until I could stand again on my own.

Most of the patients were on medication that didn't seem to help them very much. They had tried giving me a little Zoloft, and I'd had a bad reaction to it; my whole body trembled. I decided the meds were not for me, that I had to do this on my own.

So many of the other patients seemed so lost and broken, I had to wonder if they would ever truly get better. It frightened me to see people so emotionally crippled, and although I suspected that I would never feel the same level of darkness they felt, I could relate to how they did feel, and it frightened me.

"I'm worried I'm just like them," I confessed to one of my doctors privately. "Maybe I'll always feel this way. Maybe I'll never get better." The doctor smiled and touched my hand.

"A lot of these people come and go and are constantly coming back," the doctor said. "You won't be one of them. There's something different about you. You will work through your troubles and deal with them. You will leave here, and I know that you won't be back. You will be OK."

Somehow, once I heard those words, I knew the doctor was right. I was learning to deal with all the bad things that had happened to me, and I was learning to let go of them. Sure, I had been through some terrible experiences, and I had suffered. But I had also survived.

At one point I asked myself, "Do I hate the people who did bad things to me?" And I decided that no, I didn't hate them. I didn't even know them. Once I realized that I could forgive, I knew I was healing, and I knew I would be OK.

I so desperately wanted to provide the other patients with a glimmer of hope—something to hold onto that might lead them to feeling whole. The women who were raped by priests were angry at God, and I shook my head.

My first thought of my hospital stay and resultant journey was a feeling of living in hell for ten days. Yet upon reflection, I realized how lucky I was to find God again—especially when I looked around and saw nothing but lost souls.

"You can't really blame God," I told them. "Those people who hurt you are human beings. They had a choice, and, believe me; God will take care of them."

It took me a while to step back from my own words and realize: I was urging these patients to find peace and comfort in God. And the reason I was able to do that was because I, too, had found God again. I will always keep the individuals that I got to know while I was hospitalized in my thoughts and prayers. I still wonder if they are all right now. I only hope they found strength and courage to go on.

## Feeling Strength through God's Presence

Once I realized that God was present in my life again, things started to change for me. It was OK for me to get angry about what had happened to me. And then I could let it go. I found God again in the hospital, and I felt like I could cope.

Ten days after checking myself in—ten days of rehashing the hell of my past—I was ready to go home. I felt a little apprehensive about venturing out into society at first. I worried that leaving the safe haven of the hospital might set me back again. I knew I was going to miss that place in a way. I felt safe there, and the people there had helped make me feel better.

So when I arrived in my own home, in my own bed, I felt raw, exposed, and emotionally shaky. But day by day, I soldiered on, telling myself I just needed to get through that day and that the next day I would feel better, stronger. And it turned out to be true.

I never forgot about the emotionally scarred people I got to know during those ten days in the psychiatric hospital. They were so isolated from the world, both physically and emotionally. They felt the stigma of their mental illness, the embarrassment of friends and family members, and the reluctance of others to discuss the fact that they needed to escape the world and seek treatment at a psychiatric hospital. They were aware that people assumed that they could just pop a happy pill to feel better and get on with their lives, and yet they knew, as I did, that for people buried deep within their own sorrow, medication was not always the answer.

It certainly wasn't the answer for me. I knew I was one of the lucky ones. I was able to crawl out of the misery my mind had created for me, and I continued to pray that the other lost souls I had grown to know at the hospital would also find their way out.

For years, there was a part of me that waited for darkness to fall in that same overwhelming way again. I was relieved when I reached the one-year point without relapsing, then the two-year point, and then the five-year point.

Eventually I stopped keeping track, and knew I was truly standing on my own two feet. As time went on, I became stronger than ever. I would need that strength to get through the troubled years ahead. It has been many years since my hospitalization, and I feel stronger, but I know that I will always feel thankful that I was one of the lucky ones to survive such a difficult time., I know there will be more challenges ahead, hopefully I will find strength and God beside me.

## Chapter Four: The Push to Sell a Drug at All Costs

### Dedicated to the Work

When I left the psychiatric hospital and reentered the real world in the spring of 1996, it was a relief to pour myself into my work. I hadn't been working in the company's main office in Massachusetts, for very long—less than a year—before depression had taken over and I had checked myself into the psychiatric hospital.

While I was out of work, I had called to tell colleagues I was in the hospital, but I had not provided any more information than that, and I knew they must have assumed I was at a regular hospital receiving treatment for a physical ailment.
My bosses were exceptionally understanding about my absence.

"We're here if you need us, Chris," my boss told me while I was away. "Take as much time as you need. Your job will be waiting for you when you come back."

When I did return to work after a two-week absence, I decided I should be straight with a couple of managers about exactly where I had been.

"I was feeling very badly, and I needed some time to work through my problems," I said. "I was in a psychiatric hospital."

I half-expected them to take a step back from me, perhaps question whether I was stable enough to continue working for the company.

"Well, that must have been difficult," one manager said. "I'm sorry to hear you were having a hard time. But I'm glad you're back."

Those words of sympathy and comfort meant the world to me at a time when I still felt somewhat fragile and was just looking to survive day by day. As a result, I felt a strong sense of loyalty to my managers and to the company. At the time, the fact that I had been treated with kindness upon my return made me double my efforts to work hard, in a way I felt like I was returning a big favor. Later, when I grew stronger emotionally, I butted heads with one of the managers who had been kind when I came back to work. I think she particularly liked needy people, so when I was down, she enjoyed providing a sympathetic hand. But when I became self-sufficient and started speaking up for myself, she didn't seem to like that, and she turned cold and abrupt. Years later, when I requested a sales job, she completely pooh-poohed the idea, telling me I didn't have the "personality for sales."

But I wasn't working hard only because my managers had understood about my absence. I immensely enjoyed the work. It was gratifying to feel that I was helping people. Working in reimbursement, I was doing my part to make sure doctors and patients were getting paid for an AIDS drug that was turning people's lives around.

## Selling Serostim

I worked in reimbursement for more than two years, and then in early 1998 I was offered a new position as a sales representative. At the time, there weren't that many sales reps working to get Serostim on the market, maybe as many as sixty throughout the country.

This job seemed like the perfect position for me. What could be better than selling a product I truly believed was helping to save people's lives? Besides, I had had plenty of success convincing insurance companies to reimburse the drug, so there was every reason to believe I could convince doctors to start prescribing it. I was excited to work with doctors—and perhaps even patients— face-to-face instead of over the phone.

I started out working in Connecticut, commuting two hours back and forth and sometimes spending the week in Connecticut and traveling home to my husband just for weekends. After a matter of weeks, the company switched my territory, and I was told to focus my selling efforts in Massachusetts, as well as New Hampshire, Vermont, and Maine.

My territory was a notoriously tough sell for any pharmaceutical sales rep. It's difficult to get access to hospitals, which makes it tough to find face-to-face time with doctors. Many of these hospitals and doctors already have their patients on certain drugs, so it can be hard to break in and convince them to try something new.

I spent a lot of time trying to convince doctors' secretaries to allow me a moment or two of the doctors' time. When I was unsuccessful, I would leave my card and hope for a phone call. In many cases, those phone calls never came.

And the truth was, even when we were able to bend doctors' ears, we were also hitting a wall with them because of the cost of the drug. Serostim was significantly more expensive than many of the other competing drugs on the market. A three-month supply of the drug cost about twenty to thirty thousand dollars.

We were told that the drug was intended for use in periodic three-month intervals, yet some patients were staying on the drug longer, in some cases a full year, and that could cost as much as a hundred thousand dollars. At thirty- five to forty-two dollars per milligram, it cost patients between two hundred and two hundred and fifty dollars day for the six milligrams the company recommended.

We tried to convince doctors that it was expensive in part because it worked better than any other drug. While other drugs were available in pill form that added fat to patients who were wasting, we explained that this was the only injectable drug on the market at that time that was providing patients with lean body mass. It was different, and we firmly believed it worked better. But because of the cost of the drug, doctors were saying no regularly. Besides, they said, there wasn't enough data yet to prove its effectiveness.

If insurance companies wouldn't cover it, there was no way patients could afford it. Many AIDS patients were struggling financially, barely getting by on the meager social security and disability payments they received from the government.

In the early days of selling the drug, in 1997 and 1998, I would visit eight to ten doctors' offices a day, sometimes more. Most of the time, they turned me away without a single sale. When hospitals and doctors are already locked into buying other competing drugs, it doesn't matter how well you can sell. Many doctors don't want to listen—although I ultimately found out that in some cases they would listen if sales representatives were willing to walk in and make a deal.

## "What Can You Do for Me?"

During those early days in sales, I had tried to sell the drug to a group of doctors in Rhode Island. One of the doctors looked me squarely in the eye and, without a hint of hesitation in his voice, said, "Well, if I prescribe this drug, what can you do for me?"

For a moment, I was too stunned to answer.

"What do you mean?" I asked, swallowing hard and wondering if I was really hearing what I thought I was hearing.

"There is a competing drug company out there that does a lot for doctors," he said evenly, explaining that the other company had provided money, trips, and speaking engagements in exchange for his cooperation in prescribing the drug.

I guess it should not have come as a huge surprise to me that drug companies were providing doctors with kickbacks for prescribing drugs, but still, it amazed me that this doctor spoke of these illegal activities so candidly, and without shame.

"I'm sorry," I told the doctor. "But my company doesn't do that."

In speaking those words, I felt an enormous sense of pride. I believed that I was working for a company with managers who had more scruples than those competing drug companies.

When I told my manager what the doctor had said, he looked stricken—not because the doctor wanted to make a deal, but because I had blown him off.

"We have to go back there and figure out what the guy wants," he said in a way that made me feel like I had handled the meeting all wrong. "He's a high prescriber. We need to get him to bite."

I was stunned. I had fully expected my manager to agree that the other companies shouldn't be making promises in exchange for prescriptions. I had expected him to assure me that I was right to walk away. As it turned out, other managers were dispatched to talk to that doctor, so I never had to.

That was my first exposure to the crooked world of prescription drug dealing, and it left a sour taste in my mouth.

I realized that my company and its employees were not immune to the practice of making backroom deals in an effort to drive up profits. Little did I know at that time just how rampant those illegal activities were? I also had no idea just how far the company would go, just how far it would push the boundaries of the law — even if it meant lying to and harming the terminally ill patients it was supposed to help — all to make a buck. I would find all of that out later.

But at the time, I assumed that the employees weren't providing kickbacks and making deals regularly. In those early days, my biggest annoyance was how often the company moved sales reps around. I would start making headway in one sales territory, and within three to six months, managers were moving me to a completely different area, where I had to start over with a whole new list of doctors.

Despite the obstacles we faced, I was a pretty strong seller, and sometimes I felt that it worked against me; the company would place some of its strongest sellers in the toughest territories, making it harder and harder for us to meet our sales goals.

Meanwhile, managers would hire friends and give them the cream-of-the-crop territories in Boston, and I was often sent to the outskirts of the city, including Boston's North Shore and the state of Vermont, where doctors were more conservative about prescribing new drugs.

Managers always put intense pressure on us to sell more and more Serostim. If you didn't deliver the sales figures they expected, managers threatened to take away good territories and give you less fruitful ones. And if you really fell short, you could lose your job altogether. Having been out of work, I was motivated to sell, partly because I truly dreaded the thought of ever being let go. I had been out of work before, and I had no intention of going to that dark place again.

I think I was able to sell well, because doctors seemed to sense that I believed strongly in the drug. While I know many of my colleagues used the hard sell approach, hammering in their sales pitches relentlessly, I was soft-spoken by comparison and instead did my selling by using my knowledge about the effectiveness of the drug and how it would help their patients. Many doctors outside of Boston seemed to respond well to that. Besides, I worked hard, logging long hours and sometimes working weekends. I was certainly bringing in a lot more than the forty-thousand dollars I had been making in reimbursement. As a saleswoman, I started at a base pay of sixty-five thousand dollars, but I made a lot more than that with commission and bonuses.

I was psyched to be bringing in decent money. Despite the pressures that came with the job, I was even more pleased that I was working for a company that had a drug that could help people.

## Companies Push to Sell, Sell, Sell!

In late 1998 and early 1999, when it seemed that the sales reps had maxed out on the number of new prescriptions they could sell, managers devised a new way for us to get into doctors' offices.

They decided to make us "clinical consultants" in addition to sales reps. We took training courses on how to complete a bioelectrical impedance analysis (BIA), which is designed to provide a detailed measurement of a patient's fat and lean body mass.

To perform a BIA, the patient's height, age, gender, weight, and other information are entered in a computer. The patient lies down and electrodes are attached to various parts of the body, and a small painless electrical signal is circulated. The BIA measures the impedance or resistance to the signal as it travels through the water that is found in a person's muscle and fat. This test helps to determine whether an AIDS patient is wasting.

Some insurance companies, including Medicaid, were requiring doctors to perform this test and provide proof that a patient was wasting before reimbursing for an AIDS wasting drug like Serostim. Company instructed us to fill out the necessary medical forms for doctors and ask the doctors to sign them.

So, in addition to selling the drug, we were now sent out with new marching orders to sell doctors on the idea of administering BIAs to their AIDS patients as well. Some doctors found this testing attractive for one main reason: we would do the BIA testing, and the doctors would get reimbursed for the test by insurance companies. So, basically the doctors were in the fortunate position of getting paid for a test that someone else performed for them.

In fact, sometimes the company would offer certain high-prescribing doctors special deals. If a doctor wrote a certain number of scripts, or would give the doctor's office a free BIA machine, worth something like two thousand dollars. I was never asked to offer that special; Company saved that promotion for its super heavy-hitter salespeople.

## Patients' Safety

But still, we salespeople were being asked to cross a certain line. We went from selling a drug to doctors to dealing directly with patients. And not only were we speaking with patients, we were performing tests that required us to put EKG electrodes on their hands and feet. A lot of the patients had full-blown AIDS, with all the symptoms, including sores all over their bodies.

I was careful not to touch their sores, but I have to admit: I didn't always wear gloves when I was working with patients. So many of them seemed so fragile emotionally, and I was worried that if I pulled out a pair of gloves and smacked them on, it would send these patients the message that they were diseased, and that I was afraid of touching them.

I knew I was taking a chance, and it was probably pretty stupid of me not to take precautions to protect myself from getting infected. But I honestly felt that these patients were already being shunned by so many people — even family members and friends in some cases — and I didn't want to be yet another person who made them feel horrible about their situation.

Their feelings really mattered to me. I felt that medical gloves were just a reminder to these patients that they were different from the rest of us, that they were people everyone should avoid, and so I chose instead to use my own two hands to deliver the warmth of physical contact, however brief.

But the bigger question was this: was it appropriate for us to be handling patients? Forget about the fact that we could have been exposing ourselves to a deadly disease, but what about the patients? Their lives were on the line, and I'm sure they were expecting only medical professionals to perform medical tests, and we were salespeople.

Although I had some qualms about it, I personally felt OK about performing the tests, maybe because my background was in the medical field and I had dealt directly with patients before. Plus I was comfortable doing the tests after the training I had received. Yet I know some of my sales colleagues with little or no medical background were clearly uncomfortable about performing the tests, even after receiving training.

However, the BIA test did open doors that had been previously closed, so the company viewed the tests as crucial. Doctors were agreeing to the BIA testing, and I held BIA clinics every couple of weeks on a regular basis at twenty-five to thirty doctors' offices for hundreds of patients. I still couldn't stomach a hard sell — for neither the drug nor the test — but when patients were wasting, I could see it. And I was glad we had a test to confirm the problem as well as a drug to treat it. But just because we had the BIA test and an effective drug didn't mean doctors would necessarily order Serostim for their wasting patients. And even if the doctors agreed to prescribe it, they still had to get the patients' approval as well as the approval of insurance companies — and that wasn't always a given with a brand-new drug.

Insurance companies would require that we showed a certain percentage of wasting in patients — and every state had different requirements. I was working six, sometimes seven days a week, and at the end of many workdays, I went home knowing no Serostim scripts had been written. In a good week, I might get two or three orders.

That changed, though. Shortly after we started doing BIAs, we got word that Serostim had received an incremental approval. This allowed people on Medicaid to take the drug, as the government was more likely to cover the cost.

This approval acted like a green light for a drug that had been barely eking by. Suddenly doctors and their AIDS patients were clamoring for it, and we salespeople watched in amazement as our sales figures skyrocketed.

A company vice president provided the sales force with a new goal: Sell two hundred million worth of Serostim in a year; it was a huge increase from the prior year.

## Sales Perks

The Company was in fact selling a lot of Serostim. According to the company's 1999 annual report, Serostim was provided to 16 percent of the approximately 110,000 people in the United States who were suffering from AIDS-associated wasting.

During our push to sell, sell, sell—and sell big—the company set up quarterly staff meetings at spas and elite resorts in California, New York, Florida, New Jersey, Philadelphia, Arizona, and Las Vegas, states where we were likely to sell a lot of the drug and get reimbursed generously. Company managers arranged for limos to take us to and from the airport, and they put us up in fancy hotel rooms that cost up to three hundred dollars a night.

If you hobnobbed with company bigwigs at night and drank heavily, you might get a better sales territory. I couldn't bring myself to schmooze like that, so I would attend the meetings and head to bed early, knowing that might be received as some kind of snub,        but I was determined to focus on doing my job well.

The company made it known that the top sellers would be rewarded generously with ten-thousand-dollar bonuses, leather coats, tennis bracelets, and all-expense paid trips to Europe. The increased pressure to sell, along with all the perks that went along with selling, led managers to hire a whole new breed of salespeople—in many cases, their buddies. We were seeing some real sleaze balls coming in with questionable sales techniques, and yet the company treated these guys like kings because they were selling like mad and bringing in big bucks for the company.

At one point, my boss flew me to New Jersey to work with a sales rep that was considered a cream-of-the- crop sales guy. He figured I could pick up some tips about selling the drug.

"You need to learn how to be more aggressive," my boss told me. "You're not pushing the doctors enough."

So I found myself getting roped into a meeting with a fellow salesman and a doctor who was one of the company's high prescribers. The salesman told me before the meeting that the company had already sent this doctor, his family, and even his nanny to Cannes, an all-expense paid trip, in return for the doctor's speech at our conference.

Paying doctors stipends in return for speaking engagements is legal, and the company found ways to make those trips sweet for the doctors who participated, all with the hope that the company's true payback would come in the form of more patient prescriptions. So we went to a famous HIV clinic in New Jersey, and we took one of the doctors out to lunch at a ritzy restaurant. I sat back to watch this top-notch salesman in action.

This guy was considered one of the company's elite sellers. I heard these guys would do whatever it took to get a sale. They would even pick up the drugs for patients who couldn't get to pharmacies easily. This salesman was probably pulling in two hundred thousand dollars a year as his base salary.

The salesman started out by discussing the benefits of Serostim, and the doctor listened quietly, noncommittal. Near the end of the meeting, the salesman brought out the big guns. "Listen," he said, leaning forward. "We have a new program going on right now. We can pay you a certain amount of money for every patient you put on Serostim."

*A new program,* I thought. *I didn't know about any such program.*

"We have already done this for other doctors," the salesman was saying. "I think you'll be as pleased as they are."

"OK," the doctor said. His answer was a little ambiguous. He didn't agree to the deal on the spot, but he also didn't seem disturbed to hear about this so-called program that we all knew was illegal.

I sat there, frozen.

*Wow, I can't believe this,* I thought. *So this was how these salespeople were pulling in so many prescriptions.*

## Bribes for Scripts

Although some doctors clearly jumped at these bribes, others responded with shock and disgust. Around the same time as the New Jersey trip, my boss brought me into a meeting at a community health center in Lynn, Massachusetts. We met with a case manager at the medical center.

My boss again started with a typical sales pitch, and when the case manager wasn't immediately jumping at it, he pulled out his spiel: "You tell me how many clients you can put on this drug right now, and I'll send you off to a nursing convention in Florida right away."

The case manager seemed surprised. "What do you mean?" she asked. "I don't even have the authority to prescribe. That's up to the doctor."

The case manager kept a pretty good poker face during the meeting, but I could tell she was uncomfortable with the conversation.

Outside the meeting room, the case manager and I had a few moments alone.

"You know, your boss just offered me a bribe," she said quietly.

"I know. I don't know why he would say something like that," I said. "I'm really sorry."

That boss later resigned, probably under pressure, and was given a large severance. The government suspected he was involved in a Medicaid fraud complaint in New Jersey, and the government had advised our company to let him go.

The doctors weren't the only ones feeling the brunt of our questionable sales tactics. Because our salespeople were doing BIAs, the company had sales reps dress in white jackets—jackets that looked an awful lot like the medical garb doctors wore—and these sales reps were urging patients to take Serostim. An AIDS patient desperate to feel better who didn't ask questions might believe that these sales reps were actually doctors performing the BIAs and recommending the drug.

In addition, salespeople were going into patients' records, taking a look to see if a doctor's AIDS patients had lost weight so they could determine which patients were good candidates for Serostim. Doctors were letting the salespeople peek through these private medical records. We may have been called clinical consultants, but when it came down to it, we were hard-core salespeople.

I did have a medical background, but the majority of the other salespeople I knew did not. I did wear the white jacket at times, and every now and then I went into a patient's file when a doctor asked me to record a patient's BIA results. But I knew it was wrong to go perusing through patients' files. It was an invasion of patients' privacy and a breach of doctor-patient confidentiality.

Shortly after we started doing BIAs, our company discovered that there was a glitch in the computer software that was designed to tell us which patients needed the drug. Managers assured us not to worry about this glitch because it "worked in our favor," meaning it skewed the BIA information in a way that made it appear as if some patients needed Serostim when in reality they were not showing enough signs of wasting to warrant use of the drug.

I also heard of salespeople who would ask patients to strip down naked in order to get the lowest possible weight—the lower the weight; the more likely they were to get approved for the drug. And I heard that some salespeople were fudging people's weights altogether to get them on the drug. Some patients were likely getting the drug when they may not have needed it at all.

In dealing with my patients, I was careful to look for true signs of wasting—major weight loss, loss of muscle tone, among other symptoms—before telling a doctor that a patient might be a good candidate for the drug.

Meanwhile, in some states—like California and Texas— The Company was cutting deals with Medicaid to cap the total cost of the drug at thirty-six thousand dollars. So if a patient needed more than that, we were promising to cover the remainder of the cost for the rest for the year.

It sounded fishy to me, and I remember asking my boss about it.

"How can you put that cap on for some states and not offer the same deal in other states?" I asked.

I found out later that this wasn't appropriate. A regulation called "most favored nation" prevented pharmaceutical companies from making better deals in some states than in others.

And as it turned out, I discovered that even when the company promised to cap the cost at thirty-six thousand dollars per patient, the company continued to bill for much more than that—in some cases as much as a hundred thousand dollars per year. That supposed cap was a sales promise that was not honored in most states.

Everything was changing, and it was starting to get to me.

## A Shift in Focus

I had been so thrilled to get the job initially, because in those early years, I sensed that my managers and fellow employees had a great deal of compassion for AIDS patients. The company had been getting input from AIDS activists; company workers had been meeting with AIDS patients regularly to find out more about the drug's effectiveness; and there was a general feeling that we were all in this to make a large group of sick people feel better. But at some point, I felt a very definite shift in focus at the company. Suddenly it seemed that this was no longer all about fighting to make sure AIDS patients got a drug they needed; instead people were mostly concerned with making more money — more money for the company and more money for themselves.

The AIDS activists who had been so instrumental in those early years were no longer finding a voice at the company. Some of these activists had been given the drug for free, but suddenly cutting them off, telling them they were running out of free assistance and putting people on what seemed like arbitrary waiting lists to supposedly receive the drug again at a later point. I doubt anyone on those waiting lists ever received the drug for free again.

And the company was also finding a new group of patients for the drug.

Because Serostim built up a person's lean body mass and made a person look and feel better, we started seeing movie stars, body builders, and athletes getting their hands on the drug. Serostim was a synthetic human growth hormone, a performance-enhancing drug that body builders and star athletes were using, partly because it came with one important benefit: the drug was not detected in the bloodstream during drug tests.

This was a job I had enjoyed for years, but suddenly it wasn't fun anymore. It was cutthroat. Managers — who were bringing in big bonuses the more we sold — were always on our backs to sell even more, always reminding us of the perks that came with selling more and also reminding us of the pitfalls of selling less.

At times when I reached what I was originally told was my quota, managers informed me that my quota had been changed, and that I actually had to sell even more if I wanted to remain in good standing. Other salespeople on the same team had much lower quotas than I did — and yet we were all in charge of the same territory. When I complained that it wasn't fair, I received no sympathy. "I know you can do it," my manager would say.

Determined not to fail, I worked ridiculous hours—easily ten to twelve hours a day—and often visited as many as six doctors' offices per day, sometimes more. Although I was making good money—more than a hundred thousand dollars a year, with bonuses—I was also hardly ever home. My husband understood, but I could feel the strain in our relationship. I felt at the time that I didn't have much of a choice.

Other salespeople—good people who worked hard but were not measuring up to the company's standards—were given warnings, transferred to junky territories, or laid off. A couple of my friends lost their jobs, and it hit me hard. More than once, a manager would ask me to deliver Serostim milligrams for an employee who had been let go.

## Talking to Upper Management about Sleazy Sales Tactics

We were hearing more and more about "thinking outside the box"—which we knew was code for making deals with doctors.

There were times when I questioned whether I should stick with the job. Although I never offered bribes or cut any deals with doctors—and I made it clear to my managers that I was not willing to do so—I was uncomfortable with the sales atmosphere I had become a part of. I knew what other salespeople were doing was wrong, and it bugged me to my core.

I tried going to upper management once or twice about the sleazy sales tactics.

"Do you know how some of these sales reps are selling the drug?" I asked a manager once. "I heard someone offer doctors money in exchange for prescriptions."

"Maybe you misunderstood what was said," my manager said, frowning.

"No, I didn't," I insisted. "I think something should be done. Some of these people are out of control."

"Oh Chris, c'mon," he said. "Behave yourself!"

Although no one would admit it, upper management knew exactly what was going on but had decided to look the other way. They certainly weren't going to listen to me — not when the company was making big bucks.

And I admit: although I knew the company was crossing the line and most likely engaging in illegal sales activity, for a while I did look the other way as well. I rationalized it this way: I had tried to take some action by complaining to upper management. I didn't get anywhere with my complaints, but at least I had tried. Plus, I needed the job, and I figured as long as I wasn't being forced to engage in illegal activity myself, I couldn't afford to quit just because fellow workers were acting unethically or even illegally. But I also felt then that I couldn't leave because I would be abandoning the AIDS patients who truly needed me.

## Working in Maine

I got especially close to a group of about forty AIDS patients who received treatment at a doctor's office in Portland, Maine.

Two managers and I met with the doctor for lunch, and for the first time I heard one of the managers talk about setting up a new study to treat an ailment called lipodystrophy, a disturbance in the way the body produces, uses, and stores fat.

In some cases, lipodystrophy causes fat to be lost in certain areas of the body, including the arms and face; many of these patients end up with sunken cheeks, temples, and eyes. In other cases, fat builds up in particular areas of the body, especially the belly, breasts, back of the neck and upper shoulders; many of these patients have fatty growths that make them look like they have "buffalo humps" or large abdomens.

As a side effect to the antiretroviral drugs many AIDS patients took on a regular basis, patients were experiencing lipodystrophy. People were getting humpbacks—large fat deposits on the back— and even fat buildup around their hearts and other organs. Some young people were even dying prematurely of heart attacks as a result.

In addition to treating wasting symptoms, it was discovered that Serostim also provided patients with an important side benefit: It helped treat lipodystrophy by breaking down some of this fat buildup.

Serostim allowed AIDS patients to gain weight by building lean body mass, not fat, and it reversed some of the fat buildup from the other AIDS drugs. The drug was found to help with lipodystrophy — yet it was not officially approved by the FDA for that use, a key point that would come into play later.

I sat quietly and listened as these managers talked to the doctor about participating in the company's lipodystrophy study.

"You'd be great for this study because you have a lot of AIDS patients," a manager told the doctor. "Chris could do the BIAs on them, and one of your people could be assigned to do the paperwork for the study."

There was some discussion about the doctor getting paid a certain amount per patient—something like two hundred dollars, and also about getting paid for a speaking engagement if he got on board. When the doctor agreed to participate in the study, one of the managers said he would send him a check for two thousand dollars. I cringed at that but figured the doctor would complete the speaking engagement to earn his check.

I was considered instrumental to this new study, and I was assigned to stay up in Maine for the bulk of my work week. I found a room at the Residence Inn and for about seven or eight months, I worked there Sunday through Thursday each week. I would do my nine to five hours at the doctor's office, completing BIAs and working with patients, and then I would head back to my hotel to complete the paperwork.

I was not the only one conducting a lipodystrophy study. Similar studies were going on in other states as well. While I was working on the study in Maine, it was tough being away from my husband for most of the week. At times I felt lonely. But at the same time, it was nice being out of the main offices, because I could work in peace and feel somewhat shielded from the harsh pressure to sell at all costs.

And besides, it was nice working closely with patients. That's when I felt that the job was worth the trouble, that I was actually helping people and making a difference.

## The Patients Became Friends

I started getting friendly with some of the patients, most of them ranging in age between twenty and fifty. While doing the BIAs, I would start chatting with them to make them feel comfortable, and many of the patients would start opening up to me, sharing their hopes and their fears.

We'd talk about Serostim, how much better it made them feel, how excited they were to see their body mass changing. Many people started feeling better within a week of using the drug. The more I got to know the patients, the more I liked them. They were dying, and yet so many of them looked forward to each and every day.

They were thrilled with Serostim. Not only was it building up their lean body mass, but it was resolving their lipodystrophy problem. "Look at me!" I remember one man saying, pointing to his back, where he'd had a large hump that was starting to disappear. "I look great!"

I got to know one particular couple really well. One was into tanning, and he looked great. He was pleased that Serostim was helping to make him look even better. His partner also came in for treatment, and one night we went out to dinner together at a local seafood restaurant.
They were a funny couple and seemed to truly enjoy each other. I believed they were very much in love. One was probably in his early forties and the other in his late forties.

One day the younger one came in to the doctor's office and told me that after ten years together, he and his partner had parted ways. He had discovered that his partner was cheating on him. He was devastated. I let him talk and cry.

103

"You'll be OK after some time passes," I reassured him. "I know you will. Pretty soon you'll be ready to meet someone new."

"I don't know about that," he said. "I just can't believe this has happened."

He was the younger one, the buff one, and his older, geekier partner was the one who had taken off on him — the partner who had given him AIDS to begin with.

It was eye-opening to me to see these gay relationships up close. Gay couples clearly felt the same level of love and attachment to each other that heterosexual couples felt, and it was obvious that the pain of the breakup was also as heart-wrenching for gay people as it was for straight people.

I spent a lot of time with the jilted man, talking him through the pain of his breakup — until he eventually felt strong enough to move to Massachusetts, where he said he planned to start going to clubs again with the hope of meeting someone new. I was sad to see him go. He had become more of a friend than a patient.

I got to know other patients, too. I saw some every week and others every other week. I would never ask them how they had gotten HIV or AIDS, but most of the time they would share their story with me anyway — whether it was through drug use, unprotected sex, or a cheating spouse.

While many of the patients were upbeat despite their illness, others were deeply depressed.

One woman, a single mom to a thirteen-year-old boy, had contracted HIV from a boyfriend who had departed from the scene much earlier. She worried about what would happen to her son after she died. She was seriously depressed and short on money.

One day I pressed eighty dollars into her hands. "Listen," I said. "I would like to treat you to a visit at a hair salon and spa. Maybe you could go and get your hair and nails done."

I figured if she did something nice for herself, it just might be the pick-me-up she needed to snap out of her depression. At first she tried to decline the gift and give the money back. "I can't accept this," she said.

But I insisted she take it. "It will make you feel better," I told her.

"Thank you," she said, gratitude filling her eyes. I don't think it was so much the money I gave her as much the kindness that someone had heard her, understood her—and that someone was reaching out to help.

She returned from that spa visit a little rejuvenated. Perhaps it did help a little in the short term. And after that, I continued talking to her, letting her voice her fears and worries about her health, about what would happen to her son if she died. I hoped that providing a listening ear would help her through that difficult time.

But I could also tell that she was pretty far gone emotionally, and I could see that she was slipping away. She wasn't eating much of anything, and she was wasting away to practically nothing. She turned into this teeny-tiny person with little strength who showed up for her medical visits.

## Patient Losses Started to Take a Toll on Me

Eventually I heard from the woman's doctor that she had died, and I felt an ache in my heart from the loss. I asked some questions about her son and learned that he was living with his grandmother and was doing OK.

That loss reminded me of what the disease could steal away. Long before claiming a person's life, it could claim a person's spirit and will to live. The woman had been filled with so much worry about herself and her son that it had taken over and had morphed into a feeling of defeat. She had lost her battle with the disease prematurely, because she had mentally given up the fight.

Another client who had both AIDS and Hepatitis C even killed himself. The drugs these patients took often had the side effect of causing depression. And although the drugs helped people's symptoms to some extent, the patients knew they had to deal with pills and injections for the rest of their lives. In addition, after a while their bodies built up a resistance to the drugs, and they wouldn't work as well anymore, so patients were constantly switching from one prescription to the next—and then dealing with a whole new host of side effects.

Each loss hit me hard. I always wondered if there was something I could have said or done to prevent these people from giving up on life. With every loss, I would redouble my efforts with the patients who were still alive but down and out. I talked to them as long as they wanted to talk. I touched their hands to provide comfort if they were having a bad day.

Back at my hotel, I prayed for them daily—for both their physical and emotional health.

I worried about them, and when they left me at the doctor's office, sometimes I wondered if they would be dead before their next two-week appointment was up. At times I wondered if I was getting too close, too involved, too attached to some of my clients. It made losing them so much harder. But it's not as if I could control that. It may have been easier to detach myself emotionally from the patients, but it was not something I could bring myself to do.

Mostly I wanted to give all the patients hope. And I felt fortunate that at the very least, I could give them a drug that helped them feel better, helped them make it through the long and sometimes painful journeys with a disease that would most likely take their lives.

Although it was tough to see patients I got to know die, it also reinforced for me that the work I was doing was important, crucial, and, in many cases, life-saving. Some of those patients needed someone, and I was there—not only to supply a drug, but also to act as a shoulder to lean on.

## Painful Side Effects

It was worth dealing with the sales shenanigans just to see how happy these patients felt to find a drug that made them feel better. But I should clarify: the drug made them feel better to a certain point. Patients were instructed to take six milligrams per day of Serostim, but for some patients, that was way too much, and some people experienced awful side effects.

Because the drug was building up people's muscles, sometimes it caused severe muscular pain—so much so that some patients couldn't sleep at night and were debilitated.

Some patients complained that they were unable to walk. The higher the dose, the more pain they felt. I reported this awful side effect to a manager. "Tell the patients to take a painkiller," he said.

My managers seemed to feel little, if any, sympathy for the patients, and they weren't about to advise me to lower the patients' doses of Serostim — not when it was selling so well. I felt that my bosses were not listening to the patients' complaints, and they weren't taking me seriously when I tried to relay those complaints. So although the company was intent on getting patients to take the full six milligrams, I decided to take matters into my own hands with the patients I was working with.

"You can take the drug every other day, or take fewer than six milligrams every day," I would tell patients who complained of pain. "Find the right dose that works for you."

Many of them found that the drug was still effective at a much lower dose, and at that lower dose, the patients didn't experience pain. At this point, the drug was getting approved by insurance companies more often, but not always. I knew of one client who wasn't doing well, and still Medicaid kept turning down his requests for Serostim. I was alarmed, because I knew the client really needed the drug.

"I'd like to pay for the drug myself for this patient," I told a manager. The manager laughed.

"The best thing that could happen right now is that this guy will die and then we can go to the insurance company and say, 'See, this guy died.' If he dies, it might turn things around and allow us to get more approvals," he said.

I was floored at the callousness of that comment. He had no concern for the man who was suffering. Instead, my manager was hoping a person's death could be used to teach insurance companies a lesson and thereby allow the company to sell more of the drug.

**Devoted Doctors**

But in my mind, everyone's life should matter. Shouldn't we be fighting to keep everyone alive? And so I know I went beyond a salesperson's normal job duties. I would do just about anything to make patients feel better. I heard of another client who was wasting severely and needed the drug desperately, yet the client's insurance company had denied it.

"Chris, can you look around and see if you can find some Serostim for my patient?" the doctor asked me.

"I'll do what I can," I promised.

I knew it was pointless to call managers. The story wasn't likely to garner any sympathy, and therefore I figured it was unlikely the company would provide me with a supply of the drug for this patient.

So I started asking around, talking to doctors and patients, until I found another client who said he couldn't tolerate the drug because of the muscle pain. He had stopped taking it, and he ended up giving his supply to the other patient.

I would get calls out of the blue from doctors who were desperate to find the drug for their patients. I would move my schedule around and within days rush to where I was needed. Whether it was conducting BIA tests or helping the patients get the insurance approvals they needed to get their hands on the drug — I was there.

Although some doctors were involved in shady deals with drug companies, I encountered many doctors who were honest and had their patients' best interests at heart at all times. In fact, some doctors I knew well got so wrapped up in their patients' lives that they were affected almost too much. Two doctors I worked with— who were considered pioneers in HIV medicine—killed themselves years later. But at the time, these doctors and I worked well together. We were all willing to do what we could to help patients in any way necessary—on or off the clock.

## A Rare Type of Tuberculosis

In fact, at one point, a nurse practitioner at the Lowell, Massachusetts, clinic asked if I could bring some clothes to a woman who was sick. The woman was from Africa. She had sold all of her belongings and had paid someone to get her to America to treat her AIDS symptoms. But because she was an illegal immigrant with no health insurance, she was having trouble getting her hands on the prescriptions her body needed.

She was coughing as I entered her room. I administered a BIA and tried to provide some comforting words.

"You will be fine," I told her. "The nurse practitioners will take good care of you."

It was only after I left her place that I had a sinking feeling something was seriously wrong with her. I didn't realize it at the time, but as it turned out, she had not only AIDS but tuberculosis as well. Soon afterward, I discovered that I had contracted a rare type of tuberculosis from her. I was supposed to leave for a business trip to attend a sales meeting, but after my doctor examined me, he nixed that idea.

"You're not going anywhere," he said. "I should put you in the hospital and quarantine you."

I was out of work for two weeks. After working so hard, putting in so many long hours on the job, it felt unnatural to suddenly stop working and stay in bed.

At first I resisted the idea, saying there was no way I could stay away from work for that long. I tried working at home and resisted the idea of rest. Yet although the treatment was effective, my body was bone tired — not only from the illness, but from the pace I had been keeping at the company. Until I was forced to stop working for a while, I hadn't realized just how exhausted I had become, both physically and emotionally. I slept long, long hours.

By the time I returned to work, I felt refreshed, and my head was clear again. I was energized, ready to jump back into the job. I even felt better equipped to deal with all the pressure coming from sales managers.

## Little Did I Realize

Little did I realize storms were brewing — a tsunami was heading for the company and I was going to be forced to make some very tough decisions. Before this next storm was over, several lives — including Jim's and mine, Ben's and Lisa's, AIDS patients everywhere, and employees, some of whom were my friends — would never be the same.

I would be totally blindsided by the latest and devastating storm.

## It's All about Money

# Chapter Five: The Fight for Justice — at Great Personal Cost

## The Phone Call that Changed Everything

Nothing could have prepared me for that fateful phone call from a science liaison at the Company.

It was a hot and sunny day in July 2000, and I was on my way to a doctor's office to continue more BIA testing on patients when the phone rang on my company cell phone.

It was the science liaison, calling to nonchalantly tell me that the company's medical director was no longer with the company and that the so-called study he had asked me to conduct in Maine had never gone through the proper channels of approval.

I had been asked to get patients to participate in a study of Serostim's effectiveness in treating lipodystrophy. The science liaison told that the FDA had not approved Serostim for that use and the study had not been sanctioned by the Community Research Initiative on AIDS Drug Trials program, as was required. The study was not official.

Apparently some workers in the research division at the company got wind of the study after it was long underway, and they told company officials that it needed to be stopped, the liaison said.

"The medical director set up this illegitimate study," the science liaison said. "It never should have been set up to begin with — and now he has fled the company."

I figured there was no way the medical director could have gotten the study going—not only in Maine, but in several other states as well—single-handedly. I wondered how many others at the company had signed off on the study, and I wondered if they had all known it was not valid study but had gone along with it anyway only to drum up business.

This medical director was going to be a big rising star at company and bring in all kinds of money for the company, and I was sure many people applauded the study at the outset.

It was all about money and egos.

It hit me that nothing would come of the results. Patients who had participated with the hope that they might be helping other people would have to be told that the study would never be published, and that the results would not help anyone. All the work we had done was not going anywhere beyond the four walls of that room in Maine where I had conducted the BIAs. Some of those patients had agreed to take high doses of Serostim—even when it caused them pain—but they had stuck with it, because they believed that they were participating in a study that would not only benefit them but would be used for the greater good in the AIDS community for years to come.

I had assumed that the company had had the proper authority to conduct the study. It had never occurred to me that anyone within the company would stoop that low just to sell a drug. And so I went crazy.

"I can't believe the company did this!" I said angrily. "I can't believe you had me up in Maine all this time. I was getting to know the patients, working so many hours. I was invested in this. I was pumping people up and making them feel better and giving them hope, and you just smashed it."

114

As the science liaison talked about suddenly halting a drug study that patients were depending on, I was stunned into silence for a moment, my throat suddenly dry. The faces of the patients I had worked with for several months scrolled through my mind like a movie running in slow motion.

"I don't understand. How could this happen?" I asked. "We can't just take the drug away from the patients. They're depending on it to get better. We can't do this to them."

"It's OK. I'll take care of it," the liaison said in a way that made her sound tired of the conversation already.

"No, you won't," I told her. "I will stay with the patients. I will talk to them. And I will take care of this myself."

I knew I was talking to a manager in a way that could be perceived as disrespectful or unprofessional. I was letting it all spill out, and I didn't care. But it was obvious the science liaison didn't care either. Her lack of concern incensed me even more. The science liaison told me to stop the study, pack up all my paperwork, and return to the company's headquarters. "Just come back to the main office," the liaison said. "I will tell the doctors and patients that we need to stop the study. Just give me the doctor's number, and I'll notify the patients," she said.

I had been growing more and more disillusioned with the company's questionable ethics, but in my mind, this was the last straw. They had set me up to work on a bogus study? They had enlisted a doctor and terminally ill HIV and AIDS patients? This was really all about money and nothing else? Didn't this constitute fraud?

My head was spinning, but I managed to tell the liaison boldly that no, she would not be the one to inform the doctor and patients, that I would go up to Maine, face the doctor and patients and tell them we were sorry. They deserved to hear it from me, the person they had gotten to know and had grown to trust. I didn't know how I would tell them — or when — but I knew I had to be the one to do it.

"This is a big deal," I told her, close to tears at that point. Talk about stating the obvious!

But I didn't think she got it. I didn't think she understood the magnitude of how wrong this was. She was too busy placing all the blame on this medical director — who was also my former boss. Her tone was more about exposing and blaming my former boss and making him look bad, perhaps so that she could get his job. I had a feeling that this was a power trip for her. It had nothing to do with the clients.

But this liaison didn't know any of these patients. She hadn't laughed with them in high moments and cried with them in low moments. She didn't know how brave some of them were — or how broken some felt as they faced their own mortality. She didn't see how much better the drug made some feel and how much pain it caused others. She hadn't gone to dinner with them, held their trembling hands, and listened to their relationship troubles. She hadn't walked through this deadly disease with them like I had.

"I need to be the one to talk to the patients," I said. "You don't know how these patients are, what their thoughts are."

"OK," she allowed. "You can be the one to tell them."

I was shaking, but I managed to ask some questions. "What do you want me to do with all the paperwork from this study?"

"I don't want any of the paperwork," she said. "None of it is useful to us, so you can just pack it up and get rid of it."

She reminded me that my former boss had started the same study in other doctors' offices, too, and she said the company was pulling the plug on those studies as well.

## I Had to Make Things Right

I felt rage—pure, unadulterated rage—bubbling up inside me.

After hanging up the phone with the science liaison at the company, my body froze, cold to the bone. My mind went white with fury. I had to do something.

I pulled into the parking lot of a medical building in Lynn, Massachusetts. This was the same medical building where I had only days earlier tried to convince doctors to prescribe Serostim drug. Inside that building and so many others throughout the country, I thought, were patients who are fighting for their lives, patients who were counting on the medical field and the pharmaceutical field to help them.

I replayed the key details the liaison had discussed over and over in my mind, like an endless mental loop. In the most casual tone, the science liaison was telling me that the drug study I had put dozens of AIDS patients through had not been authorized by the federal government. My supervisor had set up the false study, and the results themselves had been doctored. The liaison was saying that the study had to be stopped right away and that the patients and their doctor had to be told.

117

Believe me, I was not naïve. I knew some of my fellow sales representatives would do just about anything to make a profit on Serostim. I had been in meetings with other reps and managers, and I had watched them offer doctors cash in exchange for prescribing the AIDS drug to their patients. I knew it was wrong. I knew they were bribing doctors in an effort to pump up Companies drug business—and line their own pockets with plenty of commission cash.

It all rubbed me the wrong way, and I had complained to company officials about it. Executives had always justified this behavior, pointing out that the drug was truly helping people get better. It was prolonging people's lives, and they were right about that. I was seeing the proof with my own eyes in the faces of the patients. , that still did not justify the corruption that was going on my division of the company.

But now, this was altogether different. The drug study I had been asked to conduct had all been a sham. My supervisor at Management had directed me to give patients high doses of this expensive and powerful drug. Those high doses had caused all kinds of side effects, including severe pain. Some of the patients had so much pain that they had trouble walking. And this study hadn't been authorized?

I had given so many years and so much hard work to my company, and my payback had come in the reward of working with patients, with watching them respond to the drug, with watching them grasp a small beacon of hope as they struggled to put off their inevitable demise from a horrific disease. To think that they had intentionally set up a false study, because they wanted to make money–it was too much.

And here I was, working for people who were deceiving seriously ill people. I knew I had not knowingly done anything wrong, and yet I felt sick, ashamed. This was wrong, and I had to do something to make it right. My head cleared suddenly, and I had only one thought.

## It Was Time to Blow the Whistle

I found a pay phone outside the Lynn medical building. Feeling a little paranoid suddenly that someone might hear me; I looked around to make sure no one was nearby.

I had no idea where my next phone call would lead, but I knew I couldn't use the company's cell phone to make that call. They checked phone records, and I didn't want them to see this one. Besides, I didn't want to use any cell phones, because I was afraid of getting disconnected, and I couldn't bear the thought of the phone going dead on me.

Not for this call.

I dialed my attorney, Ken, and I felt enormous relief when he picked up the phone. In one stream-of-consciousness breathless conversation, I laid it all out and told him we had to inform the federal government about what was going on.

"Ken," I said. "We have to do something." I could barely breathe, I was so worked up, but I managed to lay out the whole story — the false study, the kickbacks to doctors, and the fact that the company wasn't honoring the Medicaid cap they had promised. I told him everything. I trusted Ken. He had represented me in my case against Blue Cross Blue Shield when we had reported to the government all those overdue, boxed-up claims that were collecting dust in a storage room.
Since we hadn't been first to file a complaint, we had not received a piece of the settlement award from that case.

And right now, I felt I needed the government's help to make things right at my company as well. While I was practically hyperventilating on the phone with Ken, I was sure the Blue Cross suit came to his mind. Maybe it had even occurred to him that that suit had involved a good deal of work, and it had turned out to be fruitless, at least in terms of a payout for us. Maybe he wasn't so sure it was a good idea to pursue a whistleblower case again.

Besides, Ken was—and still is—a conservative attorney, always looking almost pessimistically at any potential case, always thinking about the weaknesses in the case and the infinity of things that can go wrong in litigation, many of which are not predictable. So Ken approached my story with a healthy amount of skepticism. Although I knew he was listening closely and perhaps considering that my complaints held merit, I wondered if he had some doubts about whether we would be successful. But even more importantly, I was catching him at a moment when he was wrapped up in a bunch of other cases that had him swamped with work.

"I don't know if they're doing anything wrong, Chris, but I'll do some research," Ken assured me. "I might be able to put someone else from my office on this to check into it and see if there is any validity to it. Right now I am tied up on a lot of other cases."

I went home that night and told my husband about both phone calls. Jim didn't know all the details, and I didn't have the energy to get into it too much anyway.

"Are you sure you want to do this?" he asked me.

"Well, it's already too late," I said. "I did it." This was how I operated. I acted in the moment and informed people later. "I'm going to fight for what's right," I told him.

"You could lose your job," he said.

"I might," I said. "I know that. But if that's what has to happen, that's fine. I have to do this."

## Taking the Complaint to the Feds

I really wanted Ken to handle the complaint, but since Ken was not available to jump on it right away, I had to figure out how to move ahead with it. I just couldn't sit and wait. I had to report immediately.

So I set up an appointment with John—another attorney I had retained to pursue a legal matter from one of my previous jobs. A friend had referred me to John, telling me that John's dad had been a prominent, highly respected judge and that John had a reputation for being an excellent litigator in court.

John did seem to know his stuff, so I had hired him to work on my lawsuit against the radiologists who had shut down my women's health business years earlier. I visited him and asked for an update on that case.

"The radiologist case is moving right along," John said.

I didn't know this at the time, but that turned out to be a lie. However, on this particular summer day, I assumed the radiology case was still humming along. And quite frankly, at that time, I didn't really want to press John for more information about that case. I had bigger, more immediate concerns on my mind.

I sat across from John in his office and quietly told him about what was going on at the company. He stared at me, enraptured and silent as I unfolded the story. By the time I finished, his eyes lit up. He had never perked up this much about the radiologist case. I knew I had his ear.

"Oh wow," he said. I could feel his excitement. "That sounds very interesting. I'm going to look into this right away."

I wasn't sure I had made the right decision to bring John into it. I had already talked to Ken about the case.

"Ken said his office was doing some research on it," I said.

"Don't worry. I'm just going to go look into it," John said. "I don't think you should wait on this."

Without letting me know beforehand, John hopped on a plane to Washington, DC two days after our conversation and started doing some research with the FDA—specifically how the company had gotten its approval for Serostim. My phone rang within a couple weeks of our meeting.

"I went to DC and did some research," John told me. "You did what?" I asked, surprised.

"I had to go to DC anyway for some other business," he said. "So I decided to look into this complaint as well."

Oh, OK," I said. I was doubtful that he actually did have other business in DC. But at the same time, I was thrilled with his enthusiasm, the fact that he was hopping right on this.

"So I came back and wrote up a whistleblower complaint against the company," John told me. "It's all ready to go. All you need to do is come in and sign it."

"Really? John, are you really sure the complaint is really ready to go?" I was impressed with his speed, and I was eager to get the complaint filed, so I made plans to get to his law office quickly.

Sitting in John's small, modest law office in Quincy, I leafed through the thin qui tam—or False Claims Act—complaint. The original complaint focused mostly on FDA approval issues and the company's failure to make good on its promise to cap the total cost of Serostim at thirty-six thousand dollars per year per patient. The complaint was later amended to include other issues: manipulating body mass test data; conducting body mass tests for doctors and having them bill the state for tests they did not perform; encouraging doctors to order more
Serostim than patients needed; and conducting a lipodystrophy study that hadn't been approved by the FDA.

However, the complaint did not include my assertion that the company was violating the most favored nation law by offering some states a Medicaid deal on the drug while failing to offer the same deal to other states. I mentioned that to John, and he brushed off my concerns, saying we could always raise that issue with the government later, and they could pursue it.

"I want to include the strongest material in the initial complaint," he said. "We can always write amendments to it later."

Much of the document read like legal mumbo jumbo to me. Other parts seemed so vague. But I was not an attorney, and I had to place a certain amount of trust in John that he was getting it right. I signed the document and felt a rush of excitement and satisfaction.

*This was really happening,* I thought. We were going to expose this illegal activity. The company would no longer operate this way behind closed doors. With the government's help, we were doing what we could to set things right. I felt a little flutter of nervousness in my stomach, but then the faces of my clients flashed before me, and I knew I was doing what had to be done.

"Please don't file it just yet," I told John. "I need to talk to Ken first."

So I called Ken again and told him that John had worked up a complaint. "I didn't want you to think I was leaving you out of this," I told him.

"No, that's OK," he said. "I'm glad to hear that the complaint is complete. You should move forward with it as quickly as possible."

"Ken," I said, "Will you please help John if he needs help?" Instinctively, I had a feeling John could use some help with this case.

"Sure, of course," Ken said. "Just call me when you need me."

John filed the complaint with the US Attorney General's Office in August 2000, and for several months, we waited. I had no idea whether the government would pursue the case. But I felt some relief just knowing that I had informed the government about what was going on. The ball was now in their court. If nothing came of it, that's life.

Little did I know then that I wasn't the only one who had blown the whistle? In September—about a month after we filed our complaint—some other workers banded together and filed their own qui tam complaint.

What I also didn't know at the time was that although we were the first to file a complaint, there was some question about whether our complaint was complete, because John had failed to file some important documentation, a "statement of facts" that the government required.

I didn't know anything about the other whistleblowers then, nor did I have a clue that John's mistake could cost us the case.

## Packing up the Study

After getting that horrendous phone call from the science liaison, I avoided going to Maine for a while. I was seething with anger at the company, for one thing, and I knew I couldn't face the doctor and clients in that frame of mind. I had to let my emotions settle down a little bit.

For about a month, I stayed away from Maine and focused on doing my work in other doctors' offices. But eventually I knew I had to get back up there and clean things up.

My boss knew that I was upset about the science liaison's phone call, and he tried a couple of times to ease my concerns.

"Don't listen to her," he told me. "I'm not sure we even need to shut down this study. I'll check it out. And even if this study won't work, maybe we can use the data for another purpose. In the meantime, don't say anything to the doctor or patients. We shouldn't put anyone on the drug for lipodystrophy. But you can keep doing your job and working with the patients who need the drug for AIDS wasting."

I knew that it was doubtful the results of the study would be used for any other purpose. I knew my boss was just trying to make me feel better. But I agreed to return to Maine and continue working with the patients. My boss and I agreed that I would not put any more patients on Serostim to treat lipodystrophy — because by then we knew it was considered an off-label use of the drug, and was not permitted. But all of the forty-three clients I was working with met the doctor's and the insurance company's requirements — at least technically — to stay on the drug for AIDS wasting, so I didn't have to pull people off the drug prematurely.

I could continue working with the patients who were taking Serostim to treat AIDS wasting symptoms, since the drug had been approved for that use. Since we put patients on the drug at different times, some were about midway through the six-month cycle with the drug, and others had just started on it. Knowing that the drug was helping people, I knew I had to stay with the patients and see them through to the end of that six-month period.

So I continued working with patients, and at first, I followed my boss's advice and kept my mouth shut about the study. At times I was tempted to tell patients that although we were keeping them on the drug, we were not truly conducting a study any longer, but I was afraid to say a word — afraid that I could get in trouble either with the company or maybe even with the government. I knew my lawsuit was sitting on the desk of a government worker, and I wanted to see how it would all pan out. Would the government decide to pursue the case? I felt that my complaint was valid, that I was bringing to light illegal activity. But it was never a given that the government could legally find fault with the company and go after them. As much as I hoped the government would take the case, I knew there was every chance the government would dismiss my complaint and decide not to look into any of it. I felt very much in limbo as I waited for word about the complaint.

Even though I didn't know whether we even had a case, I started to quietly pack up all of the records and other paperwork related to the bogus lipodystrophy study. It was all evidence now — evidence the government just might ask me to provide one day.

## Biggest Mistake of My Life?

Meanwhile, John was clearly even more restless and impatient than I was. He had turned the complaint into the government in August 2000, and as the weeks and months passed, he grew more and more antsy.

He was having some financial problems, and I felt sorry for him, so I loaned him a couple thousand dollars to help him get by. I got the feeling he wanted to speed this thing along, figuring if the government won the case quickly, he would get a portion of the settlement.

So John started calling around to various government offices to check on the case with the hope that someone would tell him that the government was interested. Knowing John, I can only imagine what he may have said during those phone conversations with government officials. He probably talked up the complaint, almost treating it like a campaign, as if he had to sell them on the idea of pursuing the case. He kept telling me he was doing what he could, applying pressure and letting the government know that we were on top of this.

"It's moving along, Chris," he said. "We have to remain patient, but I just know the government is going to accept the case."

And for all I know, maybe John's efforts did pay off.

In the fall of 2000, several months after John submitted our complaint, he got a call from the US Attorney's Office in Boston. The government was pursuing the case and wanted to meet with John and me.

John sounded ecstatic when he called to tell me the good news. I felt some butterflies in my stomach. After all, I was still working for the company, and now I would have to help the government investigate them. I was nervous, but I had to admit John's excitement was infectious, and I tried to sweep my mind of these concerns, hopeful that I would be in good hands. Yes, I was still working for the company, but surely my lawyer and the government would protect me, right? I figured I would not be fighting for justice alone.

And hearing that the government would look into the complaint made the whole nightmare — all those shady sales tactics and the bogus study — very real to me all of a sudden. It felt like I was getting confirmation that the activity I knew in my heart was improper actually was. Just the fact that the government was agreeing to investigate the complaint confirmed that I hadn't exaggerated the illegality of the company's practices.

For so long, it had felt like I was the only one questioning the company's tactics. Everyone around me acted as though things were hunky-dory, and I began to doubt whether I was seeing things clearly. So it was a relief to hear that the government had found at least enough validity in our complaint to look into the charges.

But before hanging up with John, he delivered some surprising news: "I have joined a new, larger firm, so they'll be helping us with the case," he said.

I had not seen that coming. "You did what?" I asked. "When did you join this law firm? You didn't tell me. Why are we working with these people?"

"It's OK, Chris," John said, trying to reassure me. "This is going to work out better. They're a big firm with a lot of resources. They'll help us. You'll see. It's going to work out great."

Although John tried to put a good spin on it, I suspected this was move was good for him and not necessarily good for our case. He was eager to advance his career, make more money, and gain recognition, and I think he looked at my complaint as his ticket to money and fame. Although I'm sure he knew — and the law firm did, too—that there certainly were no guarantees we would succeed.

But I tried to look at it from John's perspective. Maybe a big firm would be just what we needed. As much as I trusted John, I did have to wonder at times if he was in over his head.

"One of the partners in the firm wants to meet with you before we meet with the government," John said. "Don't worry. We'll prep you well for the meeting with the government. You'll be ready."

I was nervous as I entered the meeting at John's firm, which was in a large building in Boston's financial district. The furniture was fancy and polished. We shook hands, and the partner immediately started talking—not about the case, but about himself.

He started boasting about his involvement in different cases and various important people he knew. He talked and talked, and the more he talked, the more I grew to dislike him. He came across as arrogant, pretentious, and completely full of himself. I could tell he liked to hear himself talk. *This is the guy who will be representing me,* I thought, my stomach sinking. But I tried telling myself: maybe he'll be better in the meeting with the government. But he wasn't — far from it.

I held my coat tightly around me as I walked out of the law office building, feeling the brisk autumn air on my face. It was a gloomy day. Christmas was coming soon, and the streets of Boston were decked out in wreaths and pretty white lights. It was beautiful, but it was hard to get caught up in the Christmas spirit. As we walked the short distance to the federal district courthouse for our first meeting with the government, I was scared.

John, the law partner, and I entered a large room at the courthouse, and we came face-to-face with a room full of government officials from Boston, Washington DC, and even Pennsylvania. I was astounded to see so many suits in the room. There were at least ten people, including representatives from the US Attorney's Office, the FDA's Office of Criminal Investigations, the Department of Health and Human Services' Office of Inspector General, the US Postal Service's Office of Inspector General, and even the Federal Bureau of Investigation (FBI).

My new lawyer, the law partner, started talking — blathering really — just as he had done in the meeting with John and me. But again, he was talking about himself, not our case. He was dropping names, talking about who he knew and how successful he was. He was trying to impress these government officials. John joined in with his own self-congratulatory talk.

I sat quietly beside them, feeling a mixture of embarrassment and frustration. *When would they stop talking about how smart and important they were and get to the case?* I wondered.

Then the government officials started asking questions about the case. They addressed me directly, but my attorneys kept jumping in before I could open my mouth. In a way, that was OK with me. I was too nervous to speak anyway, so I sat quietly and let my attorneys do all the talking.

But inside, I was cringing because my attorneys weren't exactly getting the answers right. They were talking about what they thought the case was about, and yet they were twisting things, focusing too much on Companies issues with getting FDA approval and forgetting to hit the main points of the complaint. Even when they mentioned pieces of the complaint, they exaggerated things. *They're getting it wrong,* I thought.

I felt overwhelmed. I just sat there like an idiot, too intimidated to speak up in this roomful of important people. It almost felt like I was watching a movie in slow motion. Near the end of the meeting, I did answer a few questions. I was reminded before answering that I was under oath. The government officials were polite and asked gentle, softball questions. I found out later that it was typical for the government to play nice in the first meeting. It was all about making the whistleblower feel comfortable.

They asked about the BIAs and about the illegitimate study I had conducted. They asked about my role and about why I had chosen to turn in my company. I answered their questions as best as I could. They wanted a list of everyone on the sales team, so I provided that. A female assistant US attorney, Tina, did most of the talking.

"And by the way," Tina said, staring intently at me. "You should not discuss this case with anyone. You should not tell anyone the government is investigating, and you should not tell anyone about your involvement. We believe there is some validity to this complaint, and we are putting up a lot of money and manpower to prosecute this case. You have to understand that sharing any information with anyone could jeopardize the case for us. If we find out you have discussed it with anyone, we could prosecute you. So just remember, you cannot talk to anyone about this."

"Not even my husband?" I asked.

"No, not even your husband," she said. She reiterated that I could jeopardize the case if I told anyone. "This is very important," she said. "Can we get you to agree to that?"

"OK," I said nervously. "I won't talk about it with anyone."

"This investigation could go on for a long time," Tina said, "So it's important that you remain silent throughout the entire investigation."

"How long do you think the investigation will take?" I managed to ask.

There was a pause, and I saw the government officials exchange glances. "We're not sure," Tina said. "But it could take years, several years."

I quietly sucked in my breath and felt my stomach drop. I'd have to continue to work at the company for several years? All while keeping quiet about the investigation? It couldn't possibly take that long, could it? My mind was running wild, and for a moment I tuned out the conversation as my attorneys and the government officials continued to discuss the case. But at the end of the meeting, I tuned back in as I heard something that sounded important.

"We need for you to file the disclosure statement that should accompany this case as soon as possible," Tina was saying.

The law partner shot John a look. *What's going on?* I thought.

"Don't worry," the partner told Tina." We will file the disclosure statement as soon as possible, right away."

When I was alone in the room with my attorneys, the partner turned to John and started yelling.

"You haven't filed the discovery yet?" he said. "What's going on? You need to get this done! This is not a joke! You're going to work around the clock if you have to. You're not going to leave the office until it's finished, do you hear me?"

John sheepishly agreed that he would complete the disclosure statement right away. As it turned out, another lawyer in the firm worked the entire Thanksgiving weekend to finish it.

I didn't know then why it was so urgent for John to file the statement immediately. The government was simply looking for its disclosure statement — the statement of facts about the case — but the lawyers knew it was also important from our perspective, because if the disclosure wasn't filed, it was possible that our complaint wouldn't be considered complete. So if another whistleblower filed a complaint in the meantime, we might not be considered the first to file, which meant we might not be eligible for any award at the end.

But at that time, my mind couldn't really process all of the what-ifs of the situation. All I knew was that I felt sick to my stomach. The government officials had been nice, but at the same time, their questions were intimidating. And on my own side of the table, I had a couple of guys who seemed to be in this only for the money and glory.

Would these guys look out for my best interests? Did they even care that I was uncomfortable, or was I just the means to a lot of money? Was anyone looking out for me? I felt like I was being thrown to the wolves on both sides.

*What in the world have I done?* I thought. I had gotten this ball rolling, and now it was moving in directions I had never anticipated. I had no control over what would happen next. I had a bad feeling about it, and I couldn't shake it.

How long would this drag on, and how would I be affected? I couldn't imagine being mired in a complaint for years — *years!* — and having to keep the whole thing a secret. What if I slipped up? Would I lose my job over this? Could the government come after me? I couldn't help but think at that moment: *I have made the biggest mistake of my life.*

## Physical Effects of Stress

That first meeting with the government stressed me out. Up until that point, I had been able to compartmentalize my life and forget about the complaint while I worked at the company. But after meeting with the government and seeing my own attorneys in action and feeling so little faith in all of them, the consequences of my actions hit me like a ton of bricks.

Years earlier, I had experienced some health issues. In 1997, while in my thirties—before I started working at the company—I had had a throbbing pain in my arm that traveled up to my jaw. Tests revealed that I had coronary artery disease, and that my artery was more than 60 percent blocked. When it got as high as 90 percent blocked, I had to have an angioplasty procedure. But for years after that, all of my tests showed that my heart was in good shape.

Once the saga began heating up, I started experiencing angina, which caused pain in my chest and arm. I was also certain that my bulimia would be triggered even more than usual thanks to so much relentless stress. I knew I couldn't handle all of this stress alone. So I went to see two doctors— my infectious disease doctor as well as my cardiologist—and I told them about the complaint.

These doctors were honest, good guys. I knew I could trust them. Besides, they were legally bound by doctor-patient confidentiality regulations.

I had to explain the source of my stress. And quite frankly, I so desperately needed a friend I could confide in at that time. I didn't want to tell my husband too much for fear that the government would somehow find out. Besides, I didn't really feel much like talking to him about it. At the end of the day, when I was with him, I was more than happy to put the whole thing out of my mind.

So I opened up to these two doctors. They sat silently and listened to my story, and they both provided tremendous reassurance.

"I hope I'm doing the right thing," I said nervously. "I just don't know anymore."

"Chris, you're doing the right thing," my cardiologist said. "Very few people would do what you're doing. You have to expose this stuff. What the company did was wrong."

"I know," I said. "I know."

"But don't let this get to you," he said. "You need to take care of yourself."

"I know," I said again.

"And Chris," the doctor said. "I just want you to know: I'm proud of you."

My eyes filled with tears. I realized that for so long I had been acting on instinct, hoping I was doing the right thing by turning the company in but feeling so alone in soothe process.

Hearing a doctor I respected say he was proud that I was fighting the good fight went right to my heart—and gave me the strength I needed to keep fighting.

<u>Afraid of Being Discovered</u>

Within weeks of that first meeting with the government, I was doing my sales calls and was working from home when I saw an e- mail from management.

The e-mail said the government was inquiring about the company's operations, and if anyone from the outside approached us with questions—the government, the media, anyone—we should refuse to speak with them and notify someone in the company's legal department right away.

Although the e-mail's purpose was to notify employees about the government investigation, the tone was reassuring, letting employees know that the company didn't have anything to hide, and that the company was completely innocent of any false accusations. After reading the e-mail, I took a couple of deep breaths. So here it was. The government had obviously notified the company that it was investigating. Getting the e-mail made the whole investigation feel official.

I was glad that I saw that e-mail at home, where none of my fellow workers could read the look on my face. But I had to wonder: Did anyone suspect I was the one who had blown the whistle? If no one knew at the moment, would anyone figure it out at some point? Would I get fired? Between my husband and me, I was the primary breadwinner. I couldn't afford to lose this job.

I was grateful that my job kept me mostly on the road, shielded from a lot of discussions in the office about the case. I'm sure the investigation was fodder for a lot of water-cooler talk among colleagues, because occasionally I would talk to a coworker on the phone who would say in low tones, "Can you believe the government is investigating us?"

And during the sales meetings I attended, the case almost always came up. At first managers seemed to blow it off as if the investigation was no big deal.

"We're the big boys," one manager said. "You know you're a big pharmaceutical company if the government starts investigating you. The government always does this type of thing, and the investigations never go anywhere."

Coworkers mused regularly about the identity of the whistleblower, and everyone seemed to have a different guess about who they thought may have turned the company in. I chimed in, too, with my own thoughts about who the whistleblower might be. I worried that people would suspect me if I was too silent.

I worked hard at keeping a poker face, but I was sure every time I discussed the case with a coworker that "whistleblower" was written all over my face. My face is typically pretty open, and people can read what I'm thinking just by looking at me. I was worried my face was turning red, that I appeared as nervous as I felt. But as obvious as I thought I was, no one seemed to notice.

I don't think anyone suspected me in those early days. Whistleblowers are typically seen as disgruntled former employees who are vengeful, out to punish a company because they have lost their jobs or have been wronged by the company in some way.

Or they are seen as current employees with an obvious ax to grind— someone who was denied a raise or promotion, for example. For all the company higher- ups knew, I was a happy and successful employee who was selling well enough. As much as I felt as if a big red arrow with the word "rat" was pointed right at me, it was indeed all in my head, and I was able to continue working without suspicion.

## Nearly Blowing My Cover

In the early days of the lawsuit, it was still business as usual at my company. The slimy sales tactics continued, and doctors still received kickbacks for writing scripts. It bothered me.

The vice president of sales held a meeting with the sales staff, and, afterward, I stayed behind to talk with him. I told him that my boss had offered the doctor in Maine two hundred dollars for every patient the doctor put on Serostim.

"Oh, Chris," the vice president said, "You just don't like your

boss." "It's not about liking him or not liking him," I said.

"Well, Chris, you and your boss have your differences," he said. "Things will get better."

I was angry that despite the investigation, the shady deals were still going on. I took a deep breath and blurted out, "You don't know what's going on! You don't have a clue how bad it is! The people who turned in the company — they're not wrong about the bad things that are happening here!"

The vice president paused for a moment, and looked me in the eye.

"I'm sure that whatever you heard your boss say, he didn't mean it," the vice president said. "Chris, you have to learn to play the game."

I learned that senior management encouraged the companies disturbing sales practices, and I wasn't happy about it.

"No, I don't," I said. "I won't play this game." And I walked out of the office.

I knew he was aware of what was going on, but he was ignoring it, blowing me off. Even though the government investigation had begun, the company still didn't see the need to change its practices.

The vice president's comments made me angry, but at the same time, they solidified in my mind that I was doing the right thing by reporting the company.

Amazingly, even after saying my piece to the vice president, I don't think he or anyone else at the company ever considered at that point that I might be the one who had blown the whistle.

## Afraid to Tell

During the late 1990s, Lisa and I had bonded and became great friends, something we didn't have when we were children. The old resentment I used to feel for her, that I was a third wheel when I was with her and Carly, seemed to disappear. I was thankful that we had truly become friends in adulthood.

By then, our sisters Donna and Carly had moved to other states, and Lisa and I seemed to turn to each other, forming a sisterly bond that I cherished. I would pick up the phone and call her just to chat about mundane things, or we'd share stories about our marriages, her children, etc. My husband Jim and her husband Ben got along really well, too, which was a bonus.

So we usually spent every Christmas Day celebrating at Lisa and Ben's house with their two grown children, both of whom were in their twenties at that time. In 2005 the year my case against the company was just starting to heat up was no exception. At Christmas dinner, we talked and laughed about a variety of things, and then Ben started talking about work.

Ironically, I had not only helped Ben get his first job at my company, I had trained him. From there, Ben had moved up the ranks quickly. Ben was an aggressive worker and was ambitious, eager to take on new responsibilities.

Six months after he was hired, he became my manager in reimbursement. He later worked in the company's government affairs office for a while, and then was promoted as an assistant in government affairs. After a short period of time, he was named head of government affairs and was put in charge of national accounts. He was rubbing elbows with the head honchos at the company, and I knew he had their ear. In fact, as it turned out, he was working directly with legal team in its defense against the government's lawsuit— my lawsuit.

The government is really snooping around a lot Ben said. "They're requesting all kinds of information. We can tell from the types of things they're looking for that it must have been someone inside the company who contacted them."

"Really?" I said, keeping my eyes on my plate, concerned that my face might reveal the truth. I wanted so badly to tell him I was the whistleblower, right then and there. And I wanted to tell him that he needed to be careful.

"But this lawsuit is ridiculous. The company hasn't done anything wrong," Ben continued. "The government isn't going to find anything. They think they've got something on us, but they don't. We have nothing to worry about." Ben was a dedicated and loyal employee.

I didn't know what to say. Did he really believe the company was innocent? I wasn't sure how much he knew about all the shady sales tactics I had been privy to. But hearing him side with the company, I was wary of confiding in him. If I told him I was the one who had blown the whistle and tried to swear him to secrecy, I wasn't sure he would be able to keep that secret. I was afraid I might be putting him in a very uncomfortable position, that he would have to choose between siding with me or going to legal team. I didn't think it would be fair to put him in that position, to force him into taking action one way or the other.

Besides, I was fearful. What if the government found out I had told him? The government had expressly forbidden me to discuss the case. If I told Ben, could I go to jail for compromising the case? Could the government put Ben in jail, too? He was such a hard worker and so loyal to the company; I knew even if he had seen evidence against the company, it might be tough for him to believe it. We were family, but still, I wasn't exactly sure I knew how he would react to knowing I was the whistleblower. Maybe he would think I was the one who was out of line by reporting the company. And since I couldn't be sure, I was afraid of putting him in a bad spot. Telling him would set off a chain of events that neither one of us could control.

## Coming Clean with Patients

Meanwhile, I had a job to do—a difficult one. In early 2001, I knew I had to tell the doctor and patients in Maine that the drug study was invalid.

It was indeed a blessing for me that I was working in Maine most of the time so I could hide from the lawsuit at the main office. I didn't have to attend daily meetings and hear other employees gossip about who they thought had blown the whistle on the company and where they thought the investigation was heading.

But during the drive to Maine, I felt tense, knowing that I would have to lay it all out to a doctor and patients I cared about very much. *How am I going to tell them?* I thought. *What do I say?*

It didn't matter to me at the time that I had not been privy to the deception while I was conducting the study. I worked for the company that had deceived these patients, and I felt a wave of shame every time I thought about coming clean to them. I was worried about how the doctor and patients would react.

But I finally found the nerve — and the strength — to face them. I approached the doctor first and asked to speak with him privately.

"The company is going through some changes," I started out awkwardly. "We're trying to figure out if this study was a legal study."

"What do you mean?" he asked, surprised.

I explained what the science liaison had told me — that the study had never been authorized, that the company had improperly put people on Serostim to treat lipodystrophy when the drug had not been approved for that use.

"I'm sorry, but I don't think anything will come of this study," I said. "I think it's really rotten, what they did."

And then, in my attempt to show him how despicable I thought it was, I probably revealed a little too much.

"I am taking all the paperwork from this study. I'm talking to people about this," I said. "I am trying to take care of this." I didn't tell him I had blown the whistle on the company, but I knew I was walking a thin line.

The doctor suddenly looked worried. "Am I going to get in trouble for this?" he asked.

His question surprised me at first. Wasn't he concerned about his patients? But then again, this doctor was, after all, a shrewd businessman. He had a lucrative medical practice with as many as forty employees, and he hosted a medical radio show on the side. He was a multimillionaire; status mattered to him. He drove a convertible Lexus and Mercedes; he employed servants; and he lived in a house with an elevator.

"No," I assured him. "You won't get in trouble. I will make sure you are not involved."

In retrospect, I could have blown the entire case right there If the doctor figured out that I was the whistleblower and the government got wind that I had hinted as much, they could have gone after me for compromising the case and cut me out of the investigation.

It was a terribly risky thing for me to do, and I'm not sure I was thinking clearly. But I wanted so desperately for this doctor to believe that I had not knowingly deceived him and his patients. It was incredibly important to me that he knew I was disgusted by what the company had done.

As it turned out, he may not have cared as much as I thought that the study wasn't legitimate. Maybe he was more worried about his own rear end, his own career. And I guess I couldn't blame him for feeling some concern about that.

After all, we both knew he was not squeaky-clean. I thought back to the conversation my managers had had when we were setting up the study. My managers promised this doctor two hundred dollars for every patient he put on the drug, and he was slated to receive two thousand dollars he was to receive in return for a speaking engagement. Still, I had no way of knowing whether any money ever exchanged hands inappropriately. And quite honestly, although I had assured the doctor he wouldn't get in trouble, I didn't know whether the government would go after him or any of the other doctors involved. Although I suspected this doctor may have nibbled at some of the company's sales bait, I had no proof that this was the case, and I knew I was not going to rat him out to the government. I would do what I could to protect him if it came to that. I would do my best to keep my promise to him.

But irrespective of all of that, I was still surprised the doctor had not expressed any concern for his patients.

Telling the doctor was one thing, but it was even harder to think about facing the patients who had been involved in the study. The company had essentially lied to these patients by making it appear as if they were participating in a legitimate study. I had forged close, trusting relationships with these patients, and now I had to be the one to deliver the news that this supposed study was not legitimate and the results that came from it would not go anywhere.

Remember: Serostim was an injected drug. Yes, I firmly believed that the patients who were injecting themselves with needles daily — and dealing with all the discomfort that goes along with it — really did need this medication, either to treat their wasting symptoms or lipodystrophy. I could see that the drug worked for them. The problem wasn't the drug itself: it was the pretense under which some of these patients were taking the drug, a pretense we as a company had created.

More specifically, I was worried that the patients would think I had created this pretense. I didn't know how to break the news to them about the false study without compromising our relationship. Would they believe that I had never wanted to trick or deceive them into taking this drug? The study had been going on for seven or eight months. The patients had been on this drug for a long time. One by one, I began telling the forty or so patients what was going on.

"I'm not going to keep taking measurements, because, unfortunately, this study is not going to be published," I told them. "The data can't be used. The person who set up this study no longer works for the company. This study was a mistake."

Some of the patients were clearly disappointed. Some were worried that the doctor would not prescribe the drug as much — and in fact, that was true. The doctor pulled back and made sure patients met a strict set of criteria before prescribing the drug. I knew some of the patients felt hurt, used.

And I didn't blame them. I was not the one who had invented this study, but I was the one who had conducted it— and for that, I felt ashamed, terribly ashamed.

"I thought my participation would make a difference for other people," some of the patients complained, sad to hear that the study would go nowhere. After all, these patients were faced with their own mortality, and perhaps they got a boost from participating in a study they thought would be used to help other people suffering from the same disease.

"I know," I said sympathetically. "But this is all about how you're feeling, and this medication is helping to make you feel better, so that's what is important."

I stopped short of telling any of the patients about my whistleblower suit. I never mentioned the fact that the government was investigating. But I tried to reassure them with a few simple words.

"I just have to tell you that I know it will all be OK eventually," I said. "I know it will." I wanted to believe the same thing so badly myself.

## My Legal Team

Even though I was away from main office a lot, I was still seeing more e-mails about the investigation. We received new e-mails from the company just about every other week.

The company was saying that the government might submit subpoenas for certain company records. We were told that if we received a subpoena, we should notify the company's legal department right away. Six months after our first meeting with the government, they contacted us to schedule a second meeting. I called John and told him I did not feel comfortable with the partner who had represented me at the first meeting.

"I don't want him to represent me in this case," I told John. I said that he and the partner had gotten some information wrong at that first meeting and that we needed to straighten out the complaint in this next meeting. I kept trying to tell him what was really happening at the company about the shady sales practices and the false study.

But John didn't seem to be listening. He kept turning the subject back to the FDA approval of Serostim, which wasn't what I believed the lawsuit was about.

I had an instinctive urge to fire John. I questioned whether he would present my case fairly, provide accurate information, and represent me well. But I felt sorry for John. I knew he was going through some personal trouble at the time—a divorce that was getting messier and more costly each day, and he had children who depended on him.

So against my better judgment, I kept him on the case.

John agreed to bring in another attorney, Pete, to the next meeting with the government. He also told me the government had requested that I bring my company laptop and the BIA machine I had used in Maine.

John and Pete accompanied me to that second meeting with the government inside a conference room at the federal courthouse in Boston. Again, I found myself face-to-face with at least nine government officials as well as a court stenographer who took notes by hand.

We talked about my work as a sales rep and then about other sales reps, the territories we covered, the work we did. They asked about our managers and the sales tactics we were told to use to sell Serostim. They asked me to hand over my laptop, and perhaps they sensed that I felt a little uncomfortable about doing that.

"We need to go in and check out your e-mails from the company," the government's attorney, Tina, said. "We need to get some information regarding the various contests and in-house marketing."

"But I deleted a lot of those e-mails," I said.

"Don't worry," she said. "Even when e-mails are deleted, we can usually find them on the hard drive. Nothing ever really gets erased."

They asked me to demonstrate how I used the BIA machine and how we used the results from these tests to determine which clients met the insurance requirements to receive Serostim. I told them that people from marketing team had worked with RJL Systems, the company that had designed the machine.

I told them about the accidental glitch that incorrectly determined a patient's body composition, and that the company had told us the glitch worked in our favor, so not to worry about it. I told them that doctors had received BIA machines worth over two thousand dollars in exchange for writing thirty Serostim prescriptions in a month. I told them that company had urged doctors to bill for the interpretation of the BIA test results — at about seventy or eighty dollars per test — even though the machines themselves provided that interpretation.

"Did you ever offer any kickbacks to your doctors?" Tina asked me.

"I did not," I said. "But several of my superiors offered money in exchange for scripts when I was present. They told me and the doctors it was a contest the company was running."

I tried again to bring to their attention the violation of the most favored nation law, that the company was making different deals with the different Medicaid programs in different states. But I could tell they weren't all that interested. Despite that, this meeting was going well. Pete was professional. John was under control—until the very end of the meeting.

"You know, I was wondering," John said. "When Chris has her next meeting with sales managers, what do you think about the idea of her wearing a wire to that meeting?"

I shot John a look. He had never mentioned anything like that to me before. Did he really think I would wear a wire? Was he kidding? Had he watched too many crime movies? I waited for the government officials to chuckle, to politely decline his offer. The government actually thought it was a good Idea.

"Hey, that might be an idea," one of them said. "We'll give that some thought."

*Easy for them to say,* I thought.

"Chris, you need to be careful," John said to me later. "These people at the company—they might try to hurt you, you know. Have you seen the movie *Silkwood*?

As crazy as that sounded, I did have to wonder. The company stood to lose a lot of money if the government found the company guilty of these violations. If they found out I was the one who had blown the whistle, was it possible they could come after me? I convinced myself that it was a good thing Ben didn't know about my involvement in the lawsuit against the company, because I didn't want him to be in any type of danger.

The meeting with the government and my lawyers had lasted for hours, and by the time we wrapped up, I was completely exhausted—both physically and emotionally.

## Late-Night Phone Call

I was working in Maine, away from the prying eyes of my bosses, and somehow I was able to cover up the fact that I did not have my laptop for at least a week.

I thought about the government combing through my e-mail and other files, and I wondered what they would find. But I tried to stay focused on my work with the patients in Maine and put the investigation out of my mind as much as possible.

Shortly after that second meeting with the government, I got a late-night phone call from John. It was a Friday night.

He was breathless on the phone. "You were right about them," he told me. "They're a bunch of jerks. I'm leaving the firm. I'm packing everything up this weekend and leaving the office. I'm bringing your lawsuit with me. We don't have to share any of the money with them."

"What happened?" I asked John.

John said the details weren't important, but that I should know that I didn't have to work with that firm, that he would still represent me. "Don't worry," he said.

*Don't worry?* I thought. I was worried. What would happen to my case?

"John, listen," I said. "This case is bigger than the both of us. You can't do it alone. Let's get Ken involved. I feel comfortable with him. The trust is always there with Ken. He'll help you."

John was concerned about bringing in another attorney — mostly, I believe, because he didn't want to share a piece of any award we might get in the end. But I was firm and insisted we enlist Ken's help, and ultimately John actually sounded relieved. Perhaps he had as many doubts as I did about whether he could handle this case single-handedly.

I negotiated a deal with John in which Ken would receive a small percentage of any money won. I felt that Ken should get more, but Ken assured me he was fine with the agreement.

## Pharmacy Kickbacks

In February 2001, we amended our original complaint to include a new charge, lowering the price of the drug and providing kickbacks to twelve pharmacies that prescribed Serostim.

We said the company was providing so-called rebates that were illegal, and it was our understanding that pharmacists could be fined or otherwise punished for accepting money from the company.

This pharmacy amendment was almost treated as a separate case; the government investigated both complaints at the same time. The government questioned me during meetings about both cases.

Ken joined John and me for the third meeting with the government in 2001, and the government officials responded well to Ken. They knew him and respected his reputation.

I relaxed a bit—until the energy of the meeting changed and government officials started peppering me with questions about workers I had never mentioned to them before. It was obvious they were gunning for certain managers, including some who worked in offices in other states. These questions seemed to have nothing to do with my complaint. I was confused. How did they know about these people, and why were they going after them?

But then it occurred to me: maybe they were asking me questions about someone else's complaint. It was my first real inkling that perhaps a second whistleblower complaint was floating out there along with mine. The question was, which one of us had filed first? Since the government was careful not to share information with us, we wouldn't have the answer to that question for another five years.

"I think someone else turned the company in," I told John.

"Well, we were the first to file," John said. "The government has assured me of that. They're really happy with how the case is going, Chris. They're quite gung ho."

But was that true? John said a lot of things. I was starting to discover that I could not necessarily trust his word.

I found out that he had called *The Boston Globe* to put a bug in their ear about the case and to see if the newspaper wanted to do any investigative reporting. I think he was hoping that if the government started getting questions from the media, they might speed up their own investigation.

Never mind the fact that the case was supposed to be under seal and we were given strict orders by the government not to speak with anyone about it, that we could compromise the investigation and ruin the case. Thankfully I don't think the government ever found out that John had called the newspaper. John's sense of urgency was fueled by his costly divorce. He needed money — and fast.

It was around this time that I found out from another attorney that John had dropped the ball on my radiology case. Even worse: he had lied to me about it. More than a year earlier — long before the case had gotten underway — John had been asked to file some legal documents and request an extension from the judge, but he had missed the deadlines to file those motions in court.

And so a judge had long ago dismissed the radiology case. I had invested a lot of time, energy, and money into that case. All told, I had spent about thirty thousand dollars on the case — not to mention the more than five hundred thousand dollars I had lost on my investment in the women's health center. The case had gone nowhere, because John had not done his job. He had known full well that the case had been dismissed, and yet he had told me more than once that the case was still moving along in court. Once I found out from another attorney that the case was dead, I confronted John. "How could you do this?"

"I did file those documents," he insisted. "The clerk must have lost them."

"But you knew the case was dismissed. Why didn't you tell me?" I asked angrily.

"Chris, listen," he said. "I can make a plea and try to reinstate the case."

"I heard it's too late," I said. "I can't believe you've been lying to me about that case all this time."

"I'm sorry, Chris," he said. "I don't know what to say."

I was fed up with him. I started talking to Ken about firing John from the case.

"You can tell him to stop representing you in meetings, but you have a contract with him, and you're still bound by that," Ken said.

So I reluctantly agreed to let it go. But one day after meeting with the government, we were standing outside the courthouse. John was all pumped up.

"We're going to make a lot of money off this case," he gushed. "I can just feel it."

I saw it as an opportunity. "John, if we win money from this case, I want you to pay me back for the radiology case you messed up," I said." When you get your attorney's fee, I want the first $250,000 as payment for that case. I would have won at least that much." At my insistence, John signed a promissory note.

## Company Cut Back

Meanwhile, things were getting hairy at the company.

While I was up in Maine, I learned from coworkers in main offices that the government had gotten inside and was taking files and sending them to the federal courthouse. My coworkers also told me that the company was deleting all kinds of e- mails and other files — anything that could be construed as casting the company in a negative light.

Government officials were telling my attorneys that the company was putting up roadblocks any way they could, preventing investigators from getting their hands on certain materials. When the government couldn't get something from officials would ask me if I could get it for them.

So I would quietly pull and print out documents: e-mails the company had sent out, information about the rebates pharmacies were receiving, and other evidence. I would provide the requested documents to my attorneys, and they would hand them over to the government.

The days felt like a blur, and I was growing increasingly stressed out by trying to hold myself together for the government and also work hard for the company, all the while fearful that someone at work would discover that I was the one who had blown the lid off the company's illegal practices.

During the summer of 2001, about six months into the investigation, my boss accompanied me on a trip up to Maine.

We weren't there long when he got a phone call from another manager. I could read the look of concern in his eyes as he ducked out of the room and asked if he could use another room to make a phone call.

He emerged several minutes later with some sobering news: Serostim sales had dropped. The lipodystrophy studies were not going to produce new scripts either, not with the government on the company's tail.

"The company needs to streamline the sales force," my boss told me. "We're going to have to let some people go. They're going after people who might be a problem for the company in the government's investigation."

"But don't worry," he added. "Your job is safe. You've been with the company a long time, and we know you're a good performer."

I felt a mixture of relief that my job was spared and guilt that others were being let go.

The cuts ran deep—about fifteen sales reps throughout the country lost their jobs. People waited with sick stomachs for a phone call from Human Resources. They were never told on the phone that they were being laid off. Instead, an HR worker would tell the sales reps to meet their bosses at local airports with their company cars, laptops, and phones. Once they did, their managers fired them on the spot and ordered them to hand everything over right then and there.

Some sales reps tried to avoid meeting with their bosses. One of my coworkers hid his car and came to visit me in Maine.

"I took a leave of absence from the company because my stress level is through the roof," he said. "I don't think they can get rid of me while I'm on medical leave."

He was wrong. The company eventually found him and fired him. Not everyone who got fired was involved in illegal sales activities. Some of my friends who were honest, strong salespeople were being let go.

Meanwhile, my boss's friends—even those who were not selling well—kept their jobs. And I was told my territory would change yet again. I figured my current territory was built up enough that he could hand it over to one of his buddies, so that guy could look like a good performer, while I would go to another non-performing territory to do the hard, slow work of building relationships.

My friends at the main offices told me how stressful it was there. Coworkers packed up and left; people cried at work. Stressed managers, feeling the heat from the government, clamped down on everyone. Some employees had receiving subpoenas; the company was getting them their own legal counsel.

I told John about the layoffs, that the company wasn't giving people notice or offering severance packages. Some of these people were my friends, and I hated to see them stripped of their jobs and cars with such little respect, especially when some of the shadier salespeople were allowed to stay.

"Do you think there's anything legally these people can do?" I asked John.

"Well, I have a lawyer friend who does wrongful termination suits. I can put these people in touch with my friend," John said.

John's lawyer friend did end up talking to seven former employees, and we all assumed he was gathering information and putting together a lawsuit. But weeks passed, and when these former employees called him, they got no response. Since I was the one who had put them in touch with the attorney, they naturally started calling me next.

"I don't know what to do, Chris," people were saying. "I can't reach this lawyer. Is there anything you can do? Can you find out what's going on?"

I tried to reach him as well but got nowhere. I was pretty sure this guy had skipped out on the case without telling anyone.

"I don't know what's going on with this attorney," I said.

"But you told us he could help us," some said. "You led us wrong."

I understood their anger. Many of them had families to support, and here they had been blindsided by the company and then blown off by this attorney. Maybe I should have known that if John recommended him, it might not work out. Maybe it was really my fault.

"I'm sorry," I said. "He told me he would take care of this, and I'm sorry he didn't."

The flurry of activity left me exhausted and stressed. Would these people have lost their jobs if I hadn't blown the whistle on the company? Was I responsible for all of this? I felt as if I had somehow let everyone down.

## The Government Turns on Me

At least the government understood why I was doing this, or so I thought. At least I had their support.

But in my fourth meeting with government officials, they suddenly turned on me. An FBI agent placed in front of me a copy of a written request I had made to my boss for a two-thousand dollar check to be paid to the doctor in Maine. My signature was included on the request.

"What's this?" the agent asked.

"I'm not sure," I said at first. I had forgotten all about that check, so it took me a moment to remember that this was the check the company had promised the doctor in return for a speaking engagement.

"Oh well, I believe that could be payment for a speaking engagement," I said after studying the form.

"Did the doctor ever deliver this speech?" the agent asked.
"I don't know," I said.

"We think you do know," the agent said. "The doctor either earned this check or he didn't. We should remind you that if you refuse to cooperate with us, you could be perjuring yourself here, Chris."

"I wouldn't have any way of knowing whether he actually made the speech," I explained. "I didn't keep track of those things. I was just told to sign the request, and I did."

"Why would you sign a request like this?" the agent asked his voice cold and rigid. "And why didn't you tell us about it? Are you trying to protect this doctor?"

Several government officials trained their eyes on me. Everyone looked stern, irritated.

I had assured the doctor in Maine that he wouldn't get in trouble. So maybe in a way I was protecting him — just a little. I knew he wasn't completely clean. But at the same time, I didn't have any hard-and-fast proof that he had received kickbacks for prescriptions either.

More and more, these meetings seemed to be turning into witch hunts. They probed me with questions about specific coworkers and bosses. And now here they were, targeting this doctor. I didn't want to be in a position of ratting out my friends.

In my mind, this case was supposed to be about punishing the company for the things its employees had done wrong. The company was the one that had created this dishonest climate. Why were they targeting specific individuals all of a sudden? I didn't want any part of it.

"I didn't think about mentioning the request to you," I said. "It didn't really mean anything to me."

"It's our understanding that there was some discussion with this doctor about paying him two hundred dollars per patient on Serostim. Is that correct?" the FBI agent asked. "He was receiving this money, right? Why haven't you told us about that?"

"Yes, I know that managers discussed that with him, but as far as I know, the doctor did not receive any checks from the company" I said. "I worked for him five days a week. I was at his beck and call. I think I would have known if he was getting two hundred dollars per patient from our company. Do you have any checks to prove he received that money?"

That question was met with silence—angry silence—that lasted a few moments.

"You realize you could be prosecuted if you don't cooperate with us," the FBI agent said.

"Uh-huh," I said, meeting his angry eyes with my own flash of anger. "I don't know what else to tell you. I'm telling y o u everything I know."

Tina, the assistant US attorney, later called me at home to speak with me privately. I liked her and had come to trust her.

"I know you're in an awkward position," she said gently. "I know this doctor and some of these other people are your friends, and you don't want to make them look bad. But you have to understand, when you don't tell us about something and we find out about it later, it looks like you lied to us."

"I told you from the beginning that it was not my intention to hurt anybody," I said.

"I know, Chris," she said. "But listen to me. The government is not fooling around here. They mean it when they say they'll try to prosecute you. You have to tell us the whole truth even if it's going to hurt people."

I tried to explain that I had forgotten about the check request for two thousand dollars, and that I knew the doctor had spoken on the radio about AIDS, so maybe if he mentioned Serostim, that could have justified the payment in the companies' eyes.

"Besides, I didn't do this to hurt anybody," I told her. "This is about punishing the company, not individual people. I can't be involved with going after people."

"You're going to need to be honest with us and come clean with everything you know," she said. "I'm telling you this for your own good."

Ken called a few minutes after I hung up the phone. He echoed what Tina had said—that I couldn't protect the doctor that I needed to cooperate and name names when the government asked questions.

"They're really pissed at you," Ken said. "They think you're hiding things about people."

"Ken, if I gave him the check, I assume he spoke," I said. "I don't know when these people speak. But Ken, I'm not going to screw this doctor over. I'm not doing this to take anyone down. I had no intention when I started this of picking certain people and destroying their lives. That's not what this is about. If they have names, they can ask the owners of the company about them."

"Chris, they could turn around and charge you with obstruction of justice," Ken said. "You can't hide things from them."

I was exasperated, sick of it all. "You know what, Ken?" I said. "I want to pull the plug on this whole case. I've had it."

Ken paused.

"Chris, there's no plug for you to pull," he said finally. "Once you start this process, it is taken out of your control. The government is going to investigate as it sees fit, whether we like it or not."

I was frustrated. I didn't do this to tear people down. Maybe the government was out to hang specific employees, but I wasn't going to help them send anyone to jail over this. I just wanted the company to pay back every dime it had used inappropriately.

And anyway, when did this case become all about me? I thought the government was supposed to be on my side, but here they were, questioning my honesty, my integrity. They were questioning whether they could trust me. And all the while, I was asking myself the same question: who could *I* trust?

## Sick from Stress

I didn't meet with the government all that often. Sometimes we would go six or seven months between meetings.

But after each and every meeting, I would get sick. My stress level would skyrocket even before the meeting, when I started to wonder what they might ask me, whether they would go on the attack against me. And then after the meetings, I would replay the interviews in my mind over and over, obsessing over every detail, staying up at night, worried about how it would all turn out.

The stress triggered not only periodic bouts of shooting pain from angina, but it also caused my esophagus to close up to the point where food would get stuck. I had to have a procedure to stretch my esophagus, and I had to go on meds for angina. A couple of times I wound up in the hospital for a few days, as the doctors urged me to get some rest while they worked to get my heart rate down.

*I'm young,* I thought. *What's happening to me?* Both my parents had had heart disease, and they had died young, so I knew it could happen to me, too. It was incredibly scary.

One time in Maine, I was returning to the doctor's office after a trip to the store, and I suddenly felt intense pain in my heart. It felt like a heart attack. A nurse in the office took one look at me and rushed over.

"You're white as a sheet," she said. "Are you OK?"

"I don't know," I admitted, feeling faint. *I'm going to die in Maine, where this whole thing started,* I thought.

She took me to the hospital, where doctors told me I was having intense cardiac muscle spasms, which were likely brought on by stress. My husband drove up to Maine to be with me as I rested in the hospital for a few days.

Back home, I saw my own doctors and filled them in on the progress of the investigation. It was a relief to lay it all out. They let me talk, let me cry. They never rushed me out of their offices to get to their next appointments. They were kind, and they listened. And always—each and every time—they assured me that I was doing the right thing that I couldn't let corruption win.

"You have to keep going," they said. "You're doing the right thing."

"I know. And besides, at this point," I said, "I don't have much of a choice. It appears that the case will go on whether I like it or not."

But was I really doing the right thing? I wasn't so sure anymore. I felt confused. If I was doing the right thing, why was it so hard? Why did it feel so awful? Was I jeopardizing my friends' careers— their whole lives—just to make a point? And what was I doing to myself, my health, and my relationship with my family? I was a nervous wreck—and the stress was starting to break me down both emotionally and physically.

## Top Salesperson

And yet somehow I managed to do my job—and do it well.

At one point, it was announced that I was in the "million-dollar club," meaning that I had sold more than a million dollars' worth of Serostim that year. Everyone wanted to be in that million-dollar club, and sure, I had always wanted to be in it, too. It was proof that I was a top-notch salesperson, and after being criticized for not playing the game, I felt proud that I was among the elite salespeople, and that I had gotten there honestly, by selling the drug on its merits alone.

But the victory also felt hollow.

Sure, I was selling well, yet I felt I was selling for a company that was shady, and that made me feel almost as sleazy as the salespeople who were crossing the line. I tried telling myself over and over that I was still helping AIDS patients with this drug. That's what this was all about, what this had always been about. But the investigation had clouded my view, and it was getting harder to focus only on the benefits of the drug— and of the job.

In 2001, I traveled to Florida to attend an end-of-the-year sales management conference with my fellow employees.

As we sat in a large conference room, my name kept getting called over and over as I won award after award for growing my territory quickly, surpassing my sales goals, and reaching the million-dollar club. The company awarded me a new diamond to add to a tennis bracelet I had won previously.

Then near the end of the meeting, a company representative made an announcement.

"And now, we'd like to announce the number one salesperson in the country," the man said. "This person went above and beyond the call of duty, selling Serostim in territories that are known for being difficult. I'm proud to announce that Christine Driscoll-O'Neill is our number one salesperson in the country."

As the room broke into applause, for a moment, I couldn't move, couldn't breathe. I was stunned.

But then I shakily stood up to accept my reward: an all-expense- paid ten-day trip to Europe for my husband and me. The trip was worth twenty-five thousand dollars. I should have felt thrilled and proud, but instead I was groaning inside. Most of my friends had been laid off, and I was mired in a legal complaint that was taking its toll on me.

I tried to smile and nod in appreciation. I managed to mumble a brief thank you into the microphone. But as I went back to my seat, my head was spinning and I was unable to focus on the rest of the announcements — until I heard that my brother-in-law Ben had won the same trip.

Ben was beaming at me. "This is great," he enthused. "You and Jim and Lisa and I can take this trip together. We'll tour wine country together in Cannes. We'll have a blast."

I managed a weak smile. I couldn't possibly take that trip with my sister and Ben, not with this investigation going on. Other folks had won the trip, too, including the vice president of sales. I knew they would talk about the investigation, and I couldn't bear the thought of spending ten days away with them. Not now.

## Awkward Situation

Later that night, we were at a bar, celebrating. I didn't drink alcohol, so I was sitting quietly, sipping a Coke, as other employees were tossing back drinks.

One employee said, "I wonder who blew the whistle on the company?"

I stared at him, not sure what else to say. I felt a strong urge to tell him everything right there. I could tell him I was the whistleblower and I could try to bring him into the investigation, get him to help the government with it. Maybe he would turn the company in.
Maybe he would cooperate with the government.

Ben said, "Our Company is clean; the government doesn't know what it's doing. Whoever did turn them in doesn't have a clue." I tried to keep my face blank, but I'm sure it spoke volumes. In that moment, it became clear in my mind that I could *not* tell him. I couldn't guarantee that he would go along with the investigation, whether his sister-in-law was involved or not. *He has no inkling I'm the one*, I thought. *If only I could tell him that I really did have a clue — more than a clue.*

# Chapter Six: Looking to Leave

## New Job Offer

I persuaded my doctor to write a note telling my bosses that I was too ill to take that trip to Europe. The company kindly allowed me to receive a cash payout equal to the cost of the trip — minus taxes.

Ben and Lisa tried to convince me to change my mind, talking up what a great time we would all have together, but I begged off, telling them that my cardiac issues would not allow me to go.

I was thankful to avoid it. Little did I realize how bagging that trip might affect my career? A short time later, I was passed over for a promotion as a lead salesperson because my boss said I lacked "international exposure." The job was given to a less senior, less experienced, and less successful salesperson.

I was a little miffed about not getting that job. I felt that I deserved it. And it would have meant more money and more prestige.

Around this same time, a headhunter called me and said a company that sold HIV testing kits to laboratories was interested in me. The company was based in San Francisco, so I went to a local Kinko's for a job interview over Skype, and they offered me the job soon afterward.

The starting salary was higher than what I was making at my company — plus I had the potential to earn more with bonuses. But that wasn't the main reason I decided to accept the position.

It had been a year and a half since I filed my complaint with the government, and I lived in constant fear that the company would discover that I was the whistleblower and that I would lose my job. Meanwhile, John continued to suggest that I wear a wire at work. The government was busy snooping around making everyone at the company nervous and creating an atmosphere of intense pressure and scrutiny at work. Plus, after the company had downsized, everyone was on edge. Things were getting bad, and I felt like I had to get out. How could I pass up this opportunity?

I had a new boss, a guy I really liked, and he tried to talk me out of leaving.

"We can come up with more money for you," he said.

"I'm sorry," I said. "But it's too late. With everything going on with this investigation and with the layoffs, I really don't think it's a good idea for me to stay."

"Well, if you ever want to come back, the door is always open here," he said.

I smiled and thanked him. I couldn't say the words I was thinking: I knew I would *never* go back.

## Leaving and Losing My Next Job

I left my company without fanfare. I admit I had some second thoughts. Despite how weird things had gotten there, I had loved my job. I had loved working with my patients. The corruption aside, the company's drug had helped people, and I had helped people get that drug. But I tried not to dwell on that too much. It was time to go, and I knew it.

Since I was a salesperson who worked mostly on the road, it wasn't like an office full of people was there to send me off party with a cake.

But I quietly told some of my coworkers and clients that I was leaving, and everyone was kind and wished me well. Some of them told me they wanted me to stay, but since I had another good job waiting for me, they also understood why I was leaving.

Or, at least, they thought they understood the real reason.

I started the new job in April 2002, and at first it went well. I poured all my energy into the job, determined to be as successful there as I had been before. I had an opportunity to start all over, my territory was New England. My boss visited me in Connecticut and shadowed me for a couple of days.

"You're doing a good job," he told me. "You're getting the hang of things so quickly. Keep up the good work."

But at a sales meeting, my mouth got the better of me.

Another salesman at the company was also a former company employee, and at some point people started talking about my previous company. My coworkers were well aware that the government was investigating my previous company, and I think they were curious about what was going on inside and perhaps a little worried for their own selfish reasons.

"What's it like there these days?" someone asked. "It's pretty intense," I said. "I heard about some of the practices at your previous company," someone said. "I think they were doing some pretty heavy-duty backroom deals there."

"I wonder if the government will find anything," someone else mused.

"I think they will," I said, suddenly talking without thinking. "Things aren't right there, and I'm not surprised they were turned in

My comment was met with shocked silence. My fellow salespeople and managers sat there for a moment and stared at me with funny looks on their faces.

My coworkers and I knew that our colleague, the former company worker, was being questioned by the government— and had perhaps even received a subpoena.

A manager broke the silence by asking if I thought this guy may have been involved in the wrongdoing. I felt cornered, with everyone's eyes on me.

"No, no," I said. "I mean, I really don't know, but I don't think so."

They all nodded quietly, but again, the silence was uncomfortable. I was relieved when the conversation shifted.

I realized I needed to be more careful from now on with my coworkers. I had no idea how they would react if they found out I was a whistleblower. It occurred to me that I had left the company, but I still had to worry about losing my job because of the suit. I'm sure the suit would be frowned on by virtually any employer, so I needed to keep quiet. I thought I'd feel as if I could let my hair down more at a new job, but I found out from that one meeting that that was not the case.

## The Job Is Not the Right Fit for You

However, the job was going well. I had gone through three or four weeks of training and I was starting to work in the field and gain accounts.

But then while I was on the road one day, my boss called me with some news that floored me.

"I need to ask for your resignation," he said bluntly. "What?" I asked, taken aback. "Why?"
"This job is just not the right fit for you, Chris," he said quietly.

"What do you mean?" I asked. "How can you say it's not the right fit? I have only been with this company four months, and I'm bringing in business for you already. You told me yourself that everything was going great."

"Chris," he said. "Someone at your previous company called us. They were asking questions about you."

I froze. My former employer had called my new employer? Did the company know I was the whistleblower? And if they knew, were they trying to get me fired from my new job?

"Why would they call you?" I asked. "Who called, and what did they say?"

"I didn't talk to the person, so I don't know the details," he said. "All I know is, we need you to resign."

"Well, I'm not going to resign," I said, anger rising in me. This termination was completely unfair and unfounded, and my voice shook with emotion. "You're going to have to fire me."

I was scared. I needed that job. My husband was working as a chemical engineer, making about forty thousand dollars a year, which was decent but not enough to support us. I had been the primary breadwinner for a long time. We had just bought a new Highlander SUV, thinking we could afford it with my new salary. And here I was, getting axed after a few short months on the job, and not because of my performance. I was sure of that, at least.

Desperate, I put in a call to my attorney, Ken. "What do I do, Ken?" I asked in a panic. "Can the government help me? Can we somehow prevent this?"

"I'm really sorry to hear about this, Chris, but the government is not going to be able to help you," he said.

Desperate, I called Tina, the assistant US attorney I had come to trust. Surely the government could do something to protect me, to help me get out of this mess. After all, the government lawsuit was the reason I had left my employer and quite possibly the reason I had lost this new job.

On the phone with Tina, I blurted out that my employer wanted me to leave my job. Could the government somehow protect me? Hadn't they said as much? I don't know what I expected them to do, but I was crushed by the response I got.

"That's really too bad," Tina said. "But there's nothing we can do for you."

She sounded sympathetic, so I pressed her a little bit, asked if she could talk to the others and think of any way the government could help me. But her tone turned firm. "I'm sorry," she said. "Like I said, there's not a thing we can do about this."

I hung up the phone and wanted to cry. I was there to help the government, but when the going got rough, the government was not there to help me. Was I merely a pawn that they could move wherever they liked in their little chess game, no matter the consequence?

I was able to collect unemployment while I looked for a job, but I hit wall after wall with prospective employers. A couple of times I came close to getting hired, but then a human resources official would ask about my degree. Once I confirmed I had not finished college, the job offers vanished.

## Finding a New Job

So I decided I needed to go back to college. I got a low-paying job at Macy's, took money out of my 401K, and went back to school. I immersed myself in accelerated programs at two different colleges so I could complete my degree in business management and human resources within a year.

In November 2003, as I was getting close to graduating. Another pharmaceutical company offered me a job, and I gratefully accepted it. Money was very thin at that point, and Jim and I were barely getting by. It didn't take long for me to learn that my new company also offered kickbacks to doctors; it was the same old story. I had the same visceral reaction: I was repulsed and I was tempted to report it, to find a way to correct it. But for once, I kept my observations to myself and didn't tell a soul. I just couldn't bring myself to report any more illegal activity. I had my hands full with the mess.

I was worried enough that my current employer would hear about my involvement in the case and that I could lose this job, too. It made me wonder if I would always live in fear of losing a job because of what I had done. I loved working. It gave me a sense of purpose.

Despite all the stress, working made me feel as if I was surviving it all. And having been out of work more than once, I knew I didn't want to go back to those feelings of fear and uncertainty.

But it was astounding to me that this corruption was so widespread in the industry. Even though other pharmaceutical companies were aware that the government was investigating the company, they did nothing to stop their illegal practices. I guess they stood to gain so much money from these corrupt practices that it was worth the risk of fines and other punishment.

I began to wonder, if this illegal activity was indeed so widespread, what did that say about my case? Although the government seemed intent on pursuing the case, how did I know they weren't secretly saying, "What's the big deal? This happens everywhere." Government officials had told us over and over that there was no guarantee our case would go anywhere—and there was certainly no guarantee, even if the government did go after the company, that they would win.

The case had dragged on for so long—a few years at this point— that I was starting to wonder if it would ever get resolved. I knew I certainly couldn't count on it. When it was all over, these government officials and their lawyers and my lawyers and even many of the corrupt salespeople at the company would all still have jobs. I wasn't sure I would be able to say the same.

## John Loses It

The government continued to call us in about twice a year for meetings.

Some of the meetings were cordial, and others were less so. I was wary of government officials by this point. Although I had gone into this lawsuit perhaps naïvely thinking that the government was on my side and would help me through the process, it was obvious we weren't friends. It was also clear to me by now that the government was gathering as much dirt as possible on specific employees. I heard murmurs that prosecutors might even pursue criminal charges against some of these folks, but I had no idea who they were targeting. They certainly weren't sharing that information with me.

I didn't want to have anything to do with any of that. It made me a reluctant witness when the government asked me to spill names and information that I knew they would use to criminally prosecute people. Yes, the company needed to be slapped, but I hated the thought of punishing individual employees, some of whom were just trying to keep their jobs by following these unethical practices. I knew that if anyone went to jail, spouses and kids would be left behind.

I felt any criminal proceeding would only interfere with the civil case, which was already taking much longer than I had expected. We always tried to get some information out of government officials about how the investigation was going, about where it was heading and when it might get wrapped up.

But they never shared anything with us. They were the ones who were entitled to ask all the questions, and they treated me as if I were the child who could only speak when spoken to and wait patiently without asking questions.

In fact, we didn't know from one meeting to the next whether the government would even take the case all the way, whether they would proceed with a civil action. Legally, the case had to be sealed every six months, and the government would decide at those intervals whether to continue investigating. The government continued to pursue the case, but we never knew at the end of every six months whether the investigation would go on.

"There's no guarantee this case is going to go anywhere," they would remind us regularly. "We can't tell you whether anything is going to come of this case. All we can tell you is that we are still investigating."

I was tired of having the case hanging over my head. It had been years of waiting at this point. I was tired of keeping a secret — not only from former and current coworkers but from my own family as well.

My brother-in-law Ben still worked at company and the longer the case dragged on, the worse it felt to keep that secret from him.

I wasn't the only one getting impatient. My attorney John was beyond antsy. He was continuing to do whatever he could think of to speed the case along — mostly for his own selfish need to settle the case and take his share.

He told me he had met a woman on the Internet and was planning to visit her in another state. He added that he wanted to stop off in California to speak with some AIDS activists with the AIDS Healthcare Foundation.

This group helped advocate for AIDS patients and provided medical care for those suffering from the disease. But I wasn't sure why John was turning to this group, because these advocates were not in any way directly involved in the investigation.

John sounded crazy, desperate; I tried to stop him.

"You can't tell them about the investigation," I told John. "If you do, you could be jeopardizing everything."

"I need to do some investigating myself," John said. "If I can get this AIDS group all riled up, maybe they'll start asking the government some questions. Maybe that will push this case along."

He did indeed get the AIDS group all riled up, and they started contacting government officials with questions about the investigation. The government brought some of them in for questioning, but it was my understanding that these people weren't able to help the government much, because they didn't have inside information about operations at the company. And out of some bizarre miracle, the government never found out that John was the one who had informed this group of the complaint— or if they did, they never took action against us.

But regardless, I was pretty fed up with John at this point. Thankfully his leaks to the newspaper, this AIDS group, and others had not completely jeopardized the case—at least not yet. But there was no stopping him, no containing him, and I didn't know what he might try next.

"I want to fire him," I said angrily to Ken for the umpteenth time. "I've had it!"

"But Chris, listen, you can't fire him," Ken said. "He started this case and has a contract with you."

"But Ken," I said, "You're doing all the work. John hasn't done one constructive thing for this case in a very long time."

Ken was quiet. I knew he understood how I felt — and at times I knew he got frustrated with John as well. But Ken tried to calm me down and convince me that he would do the work and that I needed to live with my deal with John. I was frustrated that John stood to gain even more than Ken did on this case — *if* we won, that is. The deal we had hammered out when the case started years earlier gave the bulk of the lawyers' share to John and very little to Ken.

"I'm fine with my share," Ken told me over and over.

"But why should John get more than you?" I said. "It's not fair. You're the one who has worked this case. You deserve more than he does. All he is doing is screwing things up for me."

"It's OK, Chris," Ken would say gently. "I'm not worried about it, and you shouldn't worry about it either."

But I was worried about it. I was furious with John. He had almost destroyed the case altogether more than once, and I felt like I was always worrying about what he might try next. I knew he wouldn't rest until the case was over — for better or worse.

When we were together, he would start talking about some harebrained idea for moving the case along. "I'm going to start snooping around," he would say. "I'm good at that." It would set me off. I was starting to scream at him like a lunatic.

After he went to the AIDS group, it put me over the edge. I had asked him not to go, and he had gone anyway, and nothing good had come from it. We got the feeling that the AIDS group was now interested in becoming involved in the case for the purpose of collecting some of the settlement money. I didn't want John representing me at the meetings with the government anymore. I didn't want to hear his musings and ramblings about how he was working on pushing the government and speeding up the case.

I decided John was losing it. The ink on his divorce papers was barely dry and already he was saying he was madly in love with this woman he had met online after seeing her only once or twice. It was also clear he was in even worse shape financially. He kept moving his law office into smaller and cheaper buildings. He was talking and acting like a desperate man. I didn't trust him anymore, and I wanted him out.

Ken suggested I hire a mediator to deal with the John situation. I couldn't stomach the thought of being in the same room with John—without throttling him—so this mediator went back and forth, meeting first with me to hear my complaints about John and then with John to get his feedback.

"I want to fire him," I told the mediator in 2004.

But the mediator agreed with Ken that I was legally bound to my contract with John. It was too late to cut him out of the case. I tried to get him to take less of any money that came our way, but John and the mediator wouldn't budge on the money. I was told John would get the share that we had originally agreed on—no matter how he behaved or what he did to jeopardize the case.

I spent thousands of dollars on mediation, and I walked away with only two assurances. John would lay low and bow out of any more meetings with the government, and he would not be involved in the related case against the pharmacists.

It was not a win at all from my perspective, but I didn't really have the energy — or the money — to fight it anymore, so I agreed to the terms. At least it would get John out of my hair in the weeks and months ahead.

I called the other attorney we had used early on, Pete, and he agreed to get back into the fray and help Ken manage the case.

### The Secret that Ate Away at Me

I had done a decent job of keeping the secret for years, but sometimes my mouth got the best of me.

At one point I was chatting with my sister Lisa on the phone and she asked what I had going on that week.

"Oh, not much," I said. "But I do have to go to the federal courthouse this week."

As soon as I let it slip, I went quiet. I closed my eyes and waited, hoping Lisa had not picked up on it.

"The federal courthouse? Chris, did the government subpoena you on the case?" she asked. "You shouldn't have to go in alone. I'll talk to Ben about seeing if an attorney for my previous company can go with you."

"No, that's OK," I said quickly. "I think they just want to ask me some questions. I'll be fine."

Lisa later told me that Ben had asked someone in the legal department if they could help me and he said that the company attorney would represent me even though I was no longer employed with the company.

"The company doesn't want people to testify," Lisa said. "Just be careful."

"I'll be fine," I said. "Don't worry. I'm sure it will just be a few questions."

My heart was pounding. How could I have slipped up like that? Although I still wanted so desperately to tell Lisa and Ben, I still felt in my heart that I couldn't.

During every family get-together and holiday celebration with Lisa and Ben, I braced nervously for the inevitable:

"It's interesting," he said once. "I have to wonder how the government knows about some of the things it knows. I really have to wonder who's talking to them."

Whenever the conversation turned to the company, I squirmed on the inside and tried to keep my emotions in check on the outside. I always tried to find a way to make some sort of neutral comment like, "Yeah, I wonder," or "That's interesting," and then I would change the subject as quickly as I could, but not too quickly.

I was filled with guilt, and my mind went back and forth. Should I tell them, or should I keep quiet? In the end, I stuck with my gut feeling to remain quiet. My fear governed that decision. I was afraid if the government found out I had told him, we could all go to jail. I would later pay dearly for keeping that secret from Ben and Lisa.

## A Long and Scary Road

I didn't know when I made that frantic phone call to Ken just how much my life would be turned upside down as a result.

That call started me down a long and sometimes scary road, one that would take several years to complete—one that would leave me at times unemployed, in failing health, and with seriously fractured family relationships.

When the battle was all over, I was left with some deep scars, and the biggest one was this: Lisa had stopped speaking to me. That's because when I called Ken from that pay phone—a phone call that started a long and ugly fight for the truth—it never occurred to me then that the government would go gunning for a certain senior official at my previous company: my sister's husband Ben.

## Worried about Ben

Although Ben remained confident that the company would prevail, I sensed that he was feeling a little concerned the longer the case dragged on.

At this time, in early 2005, it became clear that the government would also pursue criminal charges against some employees and those who took kickbacks. I knew they were initially targeting the doctor I had worked with in Maine, who had stopped prescribing Serostim shortly after I left the practice. I tried to tell the government that this doctor was not the one they should be going after, but it was obvious they were intent on seeking an indictment against him. They ultimately were unable to indict him, because they didn't have sufficient evidence.

At one point a government official asked about an e-mail that Ben had sent to the staff and that stopped me cold. "I don't know anything about that," I said.

The government officials exchanged glances. "Are you sure?" someone asked.

"Yes, I'm sure," I said. "Why? What's going on?" The government officials didn't respond.

### The Other Whistleblowers

In 2004 — four years after we had filed the complaint — my attorneys and I got word that a civil settlement was being hammered out. We were told that the company would agree to plead guilty to some charges and pay a large fine. It would be millions of dollars, although we didn't know at that point exactly how much.

Tina called Ken to let him know a settlement deal was in the works. She also wanted to let him know that other whistleblowers had filed their own complaint, and it was unclear how it would all get settled in the end.

"We've done a partial lifting of the seal on the complaint," Tina told Ken. "We need to let you know at this point that you were not the only whistleblowers. There is another group in Maryland who filed a complaint as well. We're hoping all the whistleblowers will get together and work out an agreement about who gets what."

Tina had confirmed our suspicion that there were other whistleblowers, including a colleague of mine in Connecticut who had filed a separate suit as well as a former boss of mine who had worked out of Maryland office.

It was a relief in a way to hear that I wasn't the only one who had brought the company's activities to light. I wasn't the only one responsible for all the turmoil the last five years.

And in retrospect, all of the government's questions about certain employees suddenly made a lot more sense. Some of those people were employees this former boss of mine didn't like. Yet, we were concerned. The other complaint was filed in September 2000— about a month after we filed my initial complaint. But because John had failed to file the disclosure statement with my original complaint, we wondered if we might not be able to legally claim that we were the first to file. If the government stuck to the letter of the law, was it possible that we would be shut out because our complaint had been incomplete??

My lawyers Ken and Pete held a meeting to come up with a strategy for dealing with the other whistleblowers.

"We may not get anything," Ken said. "We have to be prepared for that possibility and do what we can to get you a portion of the settlement. We should try to negotiate a settlement with the other whistleblowers with the understanding that we were the first to file—since we really were. They think we have the power. Let's try to get a deal done." After several months of talks, we reached an agreement with the other whistleblowers. I was pleased that I would receive a decent portion of the settlement.

## Criminal Witch Hunt

In the middle of the settlement talks, Tina, who had led the investigation, was suddenly asked to pick up and head to DC to work on another case, leaving the case to other investigators.

Tina was a tough investigator, but she was also fair. She and Ken had a cordial and cooperative professional relationship that helped the meetings run smoothly. When the tone had grown contentious or confrontational, it was often Tina who had stepped in to settle things down.

But now she was gone, and across the table were government officials who all seemed to be jockeying to fill her shoes as lead investigator on the case. It suddenly felt as if the room was getting crowded with egos, as if all these people were striving to make a name for themselves as the case reached its close. Their focus shifted even more further from the civil complaint we started toward a criminal witch hunt. A prosecutor I didn't like much, Ann, was busy gathering forces and evidence to pursue as many criminal indictments as she could.

You could smell Ann's career ambitions a mile away. I got the sense that she wanted to make her mark with this case, that she hoped it would be her ticket to a big promotion, more money, and more prestige. So when she was in charge, the air felt more aggressive and intense. Ann was focused on hunting down the workers she figured she could single out.

During meeting after meeting, Ann had turned to me time and time again, asking me to talk to Ben, to see if he would rat on his buddies and provide the government with more ammunition against some of the higher-ups the government wanted to prosecute.

Each time she had asked, I had politely explained that I didn't feel comfortable talking to Ben, that I didn't know whether he would want to cooperate with the government. And the fact was, I didn't trust the government. How did I know they wouldn't urge me to talk to Ben and then turn around and prosecute me for squealing if Ben decided not to cooperate with them?

Maybe I was being a little paranoid, but I just didn't think it was my place to act as their middle man. If they wanted Ben, they would have to seek him out themselves. And if the company blocked access to him, then so be it. I didn't want him to be in the position of feeling torn between loyalty to the company he still worked for and the government that wanted to bring that company down. I knew exactly how it felt to be in that position and it hadn't been fun for me. The difference was that I had started this mess and Ben had not.

In my mind, it would not be fair to drag him into this, not now, while the case appeared to be winding down.

## Threatening Remarks

But Ann wasn't taking no for an answer, and at some point she decided to stop asking and start threatening.

In 2005, I was summoned to appear before the federal grand jury to answer questions about employees the government wanted to prosecute. Ann and other government officials hoped that this grand jury testimony would lead to the indictment of some the employees. I was nervous as I showed up at the federal courthouse. These hearings were closed to the public, but that didn't quell the sickness in my stomach. Like it or not, I had to tell the truth under oath, and I knew my words could help put some of these people in jail.

Standing in the hallway with Ken, I took some deep breaths as he tried to prepare me for some of the questions I would be asked. Ken was more than an attorney to me; he had become a close and trusted friend. As my stress level grew with the case, he acted like my therapist, sometimes taking multiple calls from me each day — even on weekends — to listen to me talk about my worries and fears about the case.

A group of government investigators stood nearby in the courthouse, and I saw them glancing our way. Ann excused herself from the group and approached me.

"You should know," she said in a steely voice, "that it would be to Ben's advantage to come forward now…while he still can."

I met her eyes—that cold, dark stare—and it hit me all at once: They were going after Ben. They were putting me in the position of either getting him on our side or leaving him to be hunted down, just like they had hunted the others.

I fell apart right then and there and burst into tears.

"What are you saying?" I said, probably too loudly. "I can't believe this. I can't believe you're saying this to me."

"Calm down," she said, trying to shush me.

"I won't calm down," I sobbed. "You just told me you're going to screw my brother-in-law. What do you think that will do to him? What do you think that will do to me?"

Prior to that day, the government had never given any indication that they were interested in Ben for any other reason than his cooperation with the investigation. This was the first I'd heard that they might seek criminal charges against him. If they went after Ben, my family would think that I had been part of the operation to bring him down. It was too much to even think about.

"Ben was never one of the people you were going after," I said, practically hysterical at that point. "You said you were staying away from him. You can't do this!"

Ann seemed surprised by my reaction, as if I should have known all along that Ben's neck was on the line. She rolled her eyes at Ken, as if to say I was overreacting to her comment. How did she expect me to react? She urged me once again to "calm down" and then gave Ken another annoyed look and walked away.

"I can't believe she just said that," I said to Ken. "They're going after Ben."

"It will be OK," Ken said. But even as he said these words, I detected some worry in his eyes.

"Ken, it won't be OK," I said. "If they do anything to Ben, do you know what will happen to me? To my family?"

## Testifying in Federal Court

I entered the federal courtroom feeling shaken and scared. I was supposed to provide important testimony that could be used in the government's criminal case against former sales executives, and yet all I could think about was Ben.

Would the government really go after him, or were they just trying to scare me into involving him in the investigation? I truly didn't know.

I sat in the courtroom for several hours, answering the judge's questions in front of the grand jury. I was nervous, sick to my stomach. I wasn't out to hurt these people, but there I was, providing testimony. At one point I was asked if I had a family member who worked for the company.

"Yes," I said, my throat tightening on the words, my brother in-law Ben, "Was Ben involved in any wrongdoing at the company?"

I paused, took a deep breath. "No," I said. It was the only answer I could give—the honest answer.

## An Apology

After I testified, Ann called me at home to say she wanted to apologize for what she had said earlier. "I should not have said that to you today," she said. "I'm sorry."

As she spoke the words, I didn't detect an ounce of remorse in her voice. I suspected she had been instructed to call me, that without apologizing, she might find herself in trouble for her threatening remark.

"If you go after Ben, that could ruin my life," I said. "Do you realize that?"

"No one is trying to ruin your life, Chris," she said. "We are just doing what we have to do."

Her words didn't really make me feel better. I knew Ann was only trying to cover her butt.

But something about Ann's threat had triggered a sick feeling in me that I couldn't shake: I knew no matter how hard I wanted to keep Ben out of this, that he would in one way or another become involved. When I had started the complaint years earlier, I honestly had not even thought about Ben, nor had I considered that the government would try to use me to bring him into the investigation. And I certainly had never thought they would go gunning for him and seek criminal charges against him.

I realized that I could not control what would happen from here, what would happen to Ben. What would he and Lisa do when they found out about this? What would they think of me?

## Criminal Indictments

In April 2005, four former sales executives were indicted for criminal conspiracy in the marketing of Serostim.

In announcing the indictments, the US Attorney General's Office in Boston said these former executives had offered doctors bribes— including an all-expense-paid trip to Cannes, France—in exchange for prescribing Serostim. The attorney general's office also announced that a fifth former company executive had entered a guilty plea in December 2004 and was cooperating with the investigation.

The indictments alleged that Serostim came on the market at the same time as the advent of other protease inhibitor drugs, or AIDS cocktails that decreased the prevalence of AIDS wasting syndrome, causing the demand for Serostim to drop significantly immediately following its launch in the fall of 1996. The indictment alleged that sales executives then banded together to come up with a marketing scheme to increase sales.

At least one doctor refused the Cannes trip, calling it unethical, but about ten accepted, according to the indictments. The doctors received the trips in exchange for writing thirty prescriptions for Serostim, a drug that cost twenty-one thousand dollars for a twelve-week course. If convicted, the executives each faced several years of imprisonment and hundreds of thousands of dollars in fines.

Apparently the government realized it didn't have any evidence against Ben. It occurred to me that maybe they were never all that intent on going after Ben in the first place. Maybe Ann had just tried to make me believe they might pursue him to convince me to involve Ben in the investigation. I was relieved to hear that he was not one of their criminal targets.

Once we learned that there would be a civil settlement, the government took a long time putting together a deal. In the same month the criminal indictments came down, the company announced it was setting aside $725 million to cover the cost of its settlement with the government.

News of the case began to spread, and the AIDS group John had approached learned of the settlement. As we expected, this AIDS group sensed an opportunity and asked to get in on the settlement deal. Although this group had done very little to assist with the investigation, the lawyers advised us to work with the AIDS group, so the government's deal would not be clouded by their attempts to get money. Plus we were afraid if this AIDS group threw a wrench in the process, it would drag out the case even longer.

So the whistleblowers agreed to pay this group about four hundred thousand dollars — I chipped in my share.

Meanwhile, John had already long since departed from the scene. He apparently couldn't wait for a final settlement agreement to be reached. He went to a legal settlement firm with the agreement the lawyers had reached among the whistleblowers and managed to convince the firm to buy his share and give him money in advance of a final settlement. He then took his money, bought some land in Tennessee, and married the woman he had met online.

He did not invite me to the wedding. I later found out that John had been disbarred and was no longer legally able to practice law. John and I had parted on a sour note and had lost touch, but when I heard about his career troubles, I couldn't help myself — my heart went out to him. I knew that deep down; he was a nice guy with a good heart. Besides, despite all the hassles he put me through over the years; at some point I realized that without him, my lawsuit might never have seen the light of day.

## Whistleblower Identity Revealed

A week after the company executives were indicted, RJL Sciences and its president pleaded guilty in US District Court in Boston to charges that they conspired to sell medical devices designed to boost AIDS wasting diagnoses in order to increase sales of the drug.

Pieces of the story were starting to appear in the press, and I knew that the civil settlement deal would soon be made public. And yet, I had trouble mustering any excitement. I was anxious. Soon everyone — friends, family members, former, and current coworkers — would know that I had blown the whistle on the company.

I decided it was time to tell some of my family about the lawsuit. I couldn't bring myself to tell Lisa and Ben just yet. I had to start with some of my other siblings, hoping they would provide some of the emotional support I really needed. But most of my siblings reacted with shock and disgust. My sister Donna was the only one who told me she understood what I had done and that she would stand behind me. The others were pretty harsh.

"You really screwed Ben," my brother Andy said. "Lisa and Ben are never going to talk to you again."

My sister Carly agreed that they would be angry, and she thought they had a right to be.

"You betrayed them," she said. "Chris, how could you?"

"This wasn't about them," I said time and time again. "This was about making right what was wrong at the company."

And that was the truth. But no one in my family seemed to see it that way.

## Public Settlement

On October 17, 2005, the US Department of Justice announced the settlement, the third largest health care fraud recovery by the United States government at that time.

The company, which had moved its US headquarters from Norwell to Rockland, Massachusetts, had agreed to pay $704 million to resolve federal charges that it illegally marketed Serostim by concocting a questionable medical test for AIDS patients and for offering doctors bribes for prescribing the drug.

The medical test results signaled that patients had lost body cell mass and "were wasting, even if they had lost no weight or had actually gained weight," prosecutors said in the filing. Doctors prescribed Serostim to treat the supposed problem, at a cost of more than twenty-one thousand dollars per treatment, prosecutors said.

Michael J. Sullivan, the US attorney in Boston whose office handled the investigation, told reporters that as many as 85 percent of Serostim prescriptions were unnecessary. He said the medical testing procedure was "almost voodoo-like" and that he suspected some patients may have also suffered unnecessary side effects as a result of taking the drug.

Attorney General Alberto R. Gonzales added that the company "put its desire to sell more drugs above the interest of patients."

The Company agreed to plead guilty to two criminal counts, admitting that it had violated federal law by conspiring with medical device manufacturer RJL Sciences to market fraudulent medical devices without proper approval from the Food and Drug Administration.

Under the settlement agreement, Laboratories agreed to pay a $136.9 million criminal fine, and its affiliate companies agreed to pay a total of $567 million to settle civil liabilities.

The company also admitted that it had provided kickbacks to a group of AIDS doctors by paying for them to attend a so-called medical conference in Cannes, France in 1999 in exchange for the doctors' agreement to write more prescriptions for Serostim.

State Medicaid agencies that paid for Serostim from 1996 to 2004 would be reimbursed under the terms of the settlement. California would receive the most money, at $97 million. Massachusetts' Medicaid program, Mass Health, would get $1.2 million.

The company's lab would be banned from participating in federal health care programs, and the company would have to adhere to a "corporate integrity" agreement overseen by the federal Department of Health and Human Services for five years, officials said.

The Vice President and general counsel at the company, told reporters that the company had launched a beefed- up compliance program in 2000. "I think if you asked employees here today, they would say we have a very strong culture of compliance," he said.

The government's release noted that I had initiated the False Claims Act suit and that four other employees had filed similar suits in Maryland and Connecticut. As a result of the settlement, the release noted that the whistleblowers would share $51.8 million.

This was it. The government had slapped the pharmaceutical giant—and slapped *hard*. It was the moment I thought I had been waiting five years to witness. And yet, all I felt was unsettled, worried that now that the suit was public, everything would change.

## Broken Relationships

As I was trying to find the courage to tell Lisa and Ben, the story suddenly hit the papers, with my name in black and white. The only thing that slightly saved me from total exposure among some acquaintances and coworkers was that the settlement papers listed my married name—Christine Driscoll—and most people knew me as Chris O'Neill.

Regardless, my phone started ringing and I knew reporters from the local papers—*The Boston Globe*, the *Boston Herald*, and *The Patriot Ledger*, among others—were trying to reach me. I didn't take calls from anyone except Ken, who protected me. He told reporters I would not comment and that he would answer their questions.

The day the story came out, not only in Boston but in *The Wall Street Journal* and *The New York Times*, I called Lisa and tried to find a way to explain. But she shut me down hard.

"I can't believe you did this to us," she said, her voice tense with anger. "You used us."

"No," I said, pleading with her. "You have to believe me. I never used you."

"And then you go and tell other family members about this, but you don't tell us?" she asked. "How could you keep such a big secret from us all this time?"

I knew I should have told them before the story hit the newspapers and I was filled with guilt and regret that I had not found the courage to prepare them for what was coming. But after my siblings had reacted poorly, I was too anxious to talk to Lisa and Ben and hoped that time would help me to figure out a good way to explain everything. But waiting had proved to be a mistake—and now I would not get a chance to explain anything.

"Please let me explain," I said, tears welling in my eyes. "Please, Lisa. I never meant to hurt you and Ben."

"Well, that's exactly what you did. There's nothing to explain. I will never forgive you for this," she said, her voice shaking. "I hate you."

She hung up on me.

And then it got worse. Shortly after the civil settlement was announced, Ben was fired. He was asked to pack up his things and was escorted out of the offices on Good Friday. I tried calling Lisa and Ben again and again, and each time I was met with a wall of anger.

"You ruined Ben's career. Leave us alone," Lisa said, her voice shaking. "I never want to speak with you again."

Meanwhile, the settlement money began trickling in. I began to receive some large checks. And yet I stared at them blankly, feeling none of the satisfaction I thought I would feel now that the case was complete, now that we had won.

All of that money was in my hands. I had tangible proof that the company was paying for all it had done wrong — and yet in that moment, none of it really mattered to me, even though I had been waiting for this moment for years. I had dreamed about it, had expected to feel proud that I had helped correct this wrong. I had done it for all those AIDS patients I had worked with, and yet I hadn't worked with those patients in a long time. I didn't know if they would ever even hear about what I had done.

There was no one, not a soul, there to say, "Thank you. You did the right thing."

Instead, I felt like I had created a mess. I had alienated not only Lisa and Ben but other members of my family as well. It was an empty victory.

## Criminal Case Falls Apart

Meanwhile, after the civil settlement concluded, Ann, the prosecutor, watched as her criminal case against the company executives fell apart. The four former executives who had been indicted on criminal charges were found not guilty by a federal court jury in May 2007. The jury had clearly not been persuaded by prosecutors and returned a verdict after only three hours of deliberation.

"The speed of the verdict confirms what we believed: that this case shouldn't have been charged," an attorney for one of the executives told a newspaper reporter.

In a separate case, in October 2008, Rudolph Liedtke, president of RJL Sciences, agreed to pay ten thousand dollars and serve three years of probation for allegedly conspiring to increase sales of Serostim. I was relieved to hear that no one would do time in prison. I didn't think I could handle having that on my conscience.

## Pharmacy Case Crumbles

Meanwhile, I still had another case floating out there. Although the main complaint against the company had been settled, our parallel complaint against the pharmacies was still open.

Government officials told my attorneys Ken and Pete that they did not intend to pursue the pharmacy end of the case any further, and they explained that I had a choice: I could continue seeking a judgment against the pharmacies on my own without the government's help, or I could let the case go.

I decided to pursue the complaint on my own, largely because I felt that the slap on the hand the company had gotten did not extend to the pharmacies that had also been corrupt. I felt strongly that they should be punished as well.

It was our understanding that company gave a 3.75 percent discount on Serostim to pharmacies that still billed the government at full price. The discount was part of a system in which the company was "providing preferential pricing to a select group of pharmacies," the complaint stated. I alleged in my complaint that the company had been giving these so-called rebates to these pharmacies, allowing them to earn money in exchange for selling a certain amount of Serostim prescriptions.

It was our understanding that the company had stopped this activity after the government started investigating. While still working at the company, I had printed out a memo I had received as a salesperson from company officials that said the company was canceling its "preferred provider program" in January 2001, because the company's legal team said it violated legal regulations. I figured the government would provide us with enough other evidence from its investigation to successfully win this part of the case. But when it came down to it, once government officials washed their hands of the case, they also distanced themselves from the pharmacy case completely.

In 2004, the First Circuit Court had ruled on another case, known as the Karvelas case that created a new standard for some qui tam lawsuits. That opinion held that whistleblowers could not plead generally at the outset and then later fill in the blanks through discovery-based amendments.

Rather, a whistleblower's complaint had to rise or fall based on the information in their possession when the complaint was filed and prior to receiving any discovery.

We knew our complaint held merit, but we were afraid this new standard would have required us to provide direct evidence of these improper pharmacist claims. We knew these improper claims existed, but we didn't have copies of them.
We had no evidence that definitively proved that these pharmacists had received money inappropriately — and there was really no way for us to get our hands on this evidence now that I no longer worked at the company.

Knowing that the government had been pursuing the pharmacy case early on, we asked government officials to provide us with any evidence they had that showed a pattern of inappropriate activity. But the government was slow to respond, and in the meantime, the pharmacies filed a motion to prevent the government from providing evidence while it worked to dismiss the case.

The case was ready to go to court, and we realized we didn't have the evidence we needed. I felt that the government had essentially left us out to dry. It was further proof that the government never felt obligated to protect my interests.

Once in court, a judge applied that 2004 Karvelas decision to our case. Although we tried to argue that it shouldn't apply, the judge still balked at our lack of evidence. Our complaint was dismissed by the judge in 2007. It was bad enough that we weren't able to make these corrupt pharmacies pay for tampering with scripts at the expense of patients, but I had spent my own money on the case. It felt like a waste of time and resources.

What I didn't expect was that the pharmacies would turn around and threaten to sue me, arguing that I should pay all their attorneys' and court fees. I felt that they knew I had just won a large settlement, and they wanted a piece of it. I think it was also their way of sending a message to all whistleblowers: if you lose in your attempt to come after big business, you could get slapped in the face and be forced to pay six figures for tattling.

I was furious. I wanted to fight them as far as the case would go in court, just because it felt so wrong, so unjust for these people to not only walk away unscathed, but to walk away with some of my money. But my attorneys encouraged me to pay them and make them go away, because they were worried we might not win if their suit went to court.

"You could lose more, Chris," Pete told me. "You could lose a

lot." The pharmacies' attorneys tried to get us to pay nearly $750,000 in attorneys' and court fees. After filing an appeal, Pete negotiated with them and managed to get that number down, but it was still a huge pill for me to swallow. So between clenched teeth, I wrote these pharmacies a six-figure check.

It was a tough time for me. Yes, I had won the case, but in my quest to bring the pharmacies' behavior to light, I had lost. It didn't matter that I had been awarded a lot of money in the other case. I still felt very much alone in this one. Most of all, I was outraged that these pharmacies were getting away with this activity. I still have all the documents from the company naming
the pharmacies who were involved in the preferred provider agreement.

But how could I go complaining to family members or friends? When you come into a lot of money, you lose the license to complain. People assume you have it all. Who wants to listen to the poor rich girl cry?

## Healing

For years, my sister Lisa and her husband Ben didn't speak to me.

And the situation wasn't much better with some of my other siblings, who seemed to side with Lisa. They resented me.

Plus, I'm sure my brothers and sisters understandably felt as if they were in the middle of our conflict. Lisa's anger toward me obviously created a dilemma for them about which of us to invite to holidays, birthdays, and other family gatherings. Lisa certainly didn't want to be in the same house with me, much less the same room.

I was probably more often the odd one out, but I accepted that as my punishment. It reminded me of how I had felt growing up—I'd always felt like the odd one out. And after a lifetime of trying to fit in, of struggling to get close to my family, I felt like I was an outsider once again. Yet I had decided soon after the settlement that I would never stop trying to fix my relationship with Lisa. It was too important to me. I prayed that if she could truly never forgive me or see things from my perspective, maybe one day she would at least be able to move past what had happened, so we could be close again.

In the fall of 2009, a family member told me that a close relative of Ben's had died.

My heart went out to both Ben and Lisa, and I felt the need to attend the wake, to show them both that I cared, that I was there to support them. But I certainly didn't want my presence to create a scene or stir up any additional difficult emotions for anyone. So I made sure to keep my distance from the family by staying outside the funeral home. I figured I would stand there for a while, perhaps chat with some other family members as they came in and out, and then head on home. It had been four years since Lisa had stopped speaking to me. And then suddenly there she was, pushing open the door of the funeral home and walking outside toward me. "Hi," she said almost shyly. I was nervous; worried she had come outside to tell me to leave.

"Hi, Lisa," I said. "I just wanted to come and express my condolences. I'm so sorry for your loss."

"Thank you," she said softly, bowing her head for a moment. "I appreciate that."

We stood like that for a moment, both of us quiet. Then she looked me in the eyes, and I could see that her anger was gone. She was seeing me for the person I was again for the first time in years.

"Enough is enough," she said softly. "You and I, we need to move on."

I was almost afraid I was hearing things. Relief flooded over me. We hugged, and for the first time in years, I felt a certain tightness in my chest loosen. We were truly sisters again.

"Thank you," I said. "It makes me so happy to hear that."

Lisa smiled, took me by the arm, and ushered me inside, where the rest of the family was waiting.

## The Money Comes with a Price

As for the money I won — well, it changed my life.

For more than a year after the settlement, I continued working for a pharmaceutical company. But I ended up leaving, largely because my boss kept making annoying comments.

"I can't imagine why you would want to keep working here," he would say. "If I had your money, I would be long gone by now."

It wasn't that he was right — not at all. No matter how big my bank account had gotten, I still loved the gratification that came with working hard and earning a paycheck. But I got tired of hearing him make those remarks repeatedly. Sure, I never allowed myself to take some time off to relax and travel. I wanted to work and make a real difference. That is why One Life at a Time exists. Jim and I know we had obligations to help others with the money.

We kept our modest home in a Boston suburb but also purchased a second investment property on the beach. I enjoyed buying jewelry and some other nice things. But the highs that came with those purchases were always fleeting. We also shared our money, providing family members with help to make their lives more comfortable.

And yet, you learn when you come into money that it comes with a price. You realize when you have money, no matter how much you give, sometimes it is never enough. I am a walking checkbook to some people, a magnet to friends and family members with money problems and their subtle, or not-so-subtle, requests for help. And so that is the cross I feel I have to bear for winning this money. People treat you differently. It makes you wonder if some people are nice to you only because they hope to get something from you.

It reminded me of when I lost my money and possessions and had to start all over again. It makes you question who really loves you for *you*, not for your bank account. I still struggle on a daily basis about what I should do when someone comes to me with a financial problem.

It hurts to see all the struggles and pain when I talk with clients and middle-class individuals who are losing everything that they worked for all their life. I can only do a small part to make their lives better. I know I do not have enough money left to help all of those in need; that will always be a struggle for me.

Why is it that we do not help our own? I hear a lot about people who give their money to benefit people in other countries, but people are starving here. Who is helping them? I will continue to help those in need; I have used my own money to help those who were affected by Sandy in New York and New Jersey.

## Would I Do It All Over Again?

Ken remains a close and trusted friend, I will always be grateful to him for all the support. Perhaps because he was involved in winning such a large whistleblower award, he is contacted from time to time by people at other companies who contemplate filing qui tam complaints. Ken has never pursued another whistleblower case. Having watched what I went through, he also tells these potential clients that the process can be long and painful, the results uncertain, and, in the end, they just might regret that they ever filed a suit.

Years after the case settled, Ken called to say he had been approached by a researcher from Harvard, Aaron S. Kesselheim, who wanted to know if I would participate in a study of whistleblowers involved in federal qui tam cases against pharmaceutical manufacturers. I agreed to be interviewed.

The results of the study, which were published in *The New England Journal of Medicine* in May 2010, were fascinating. All of the twenty-six respondents said that their decision to file a qui tam action was not motivated by the potential for money; the decisive factors were instead: integrity, altruism and the concern for public health, the duty to bring criminals to justice, and the fear of being a scapegoat. Many of the whistleblowers, like me, had first tried to complain to executives within the company and were brushed off, which led them to file their suits. Some of the whistleblowers who were interviewed reported having conflicts with investigators and complained about how their lives were left in uncertainty for years while the government took a long time to investigate.

A majority said they had experienced harassment, intimidation, or other forms of pressure on the job, and some said the whistleblower complaints had ruined their careers. Some mentioned the personal problems they experienced during that time, including divorces, severe marital strain, and other family conflicts. Half reported having stress-related health problems, including panic attacks, insomnia, migraine headaches, and generalized anxiety.

Despite the psychological and financial toll people experienced, the study found that the majority of participants felt they had done the right thing for ethical, spiritual, or psychological reasons.

Yet a few whistleblowers seemed sorry they had ever filed complaints. "Honestly, I would not advise anybody to do it," one whistleblower said. When the researcher asked me whether I was glad that I had filed the complaint, I paused for a moment. I thought about all the problems the case had caused — tremendous stress, heart problems, and other health issues, and a broken relationship with my sister and her husband. And yet, fighting for the truth was the right thing to do. I didn't have to think long about whether I would do it all over again.

"Yes," I said. "I'm glad I did it, and I would do it again." The only thing I would change is telling Ben that I was going to go to the government to turn the company in for all the kickbacks and fraud in the sales department.

## Apology to Ben

Someone once said, "Time heals all wounds," and I truly hope that means Ben will accept my apology for all the pain and suffering my lawsuit caused him while he was working at the company. As much as I wanted to tell him and my siblings, I *couldn't*, and as naïve as this may sound, I actually thought the less Ben knew about my lawsuit, the more he would be protected. That is a regret I will have to live with for the rest of my life.

My brother-in-law and friend, Ben, was destroyed by the company management, and I had no inkling of this because of the rift we experienced after my whistleblower identity was revealed.

I understand from mutual friends and acquaintances that Ben was harassed at the workplace, because of his connection to me. All the time the lawsuit was going on, Ben was being held accountable for my actions, and Ben had no understanding why.

Once my identity was known to the company, it didn't take long for the powers that be to unleash their fury on an unsuspecting employee, whose only crime was that he was related to me.

What a tragedy! Ben was a great employee for the company. By his very nature, Ben is very loyal, and even though I knew what would be coming next, Ben had no idea why I was in federal court and no idea that I was going after the company.

While still employed at the company and the hint of government involvement was mentioned, it was always Ben that came to company's defense and said what a great company they were. It made me sick, but, again, I *couldn't* say anything.

For all those, and you know who you are, that think that Ben is anything but professional, extremely smart, and one of the company's best, then you need to talk to me. In war, innocent victims are considered collateral damage. In my war and the government's war against the company, Ben was collateral damage. And that will always be on my conscience.

# One Life at a Time

## Chapter Seven: Finding a Purpose

### Opening One Life at a Time

Jim and I knew we had been given a great responsibility.

We believed that God had allowed us to receive this money but for some greater purpose. So I prayed about it, prayed that we would use the money wisely and well, and in a way that would help people.

"We need to handle this money with respect," said Jim, who kept the engineering job he loved.

And in prayer, the answer came to me. Times are going to get tough. A lot of people are going to lose their jobs, and they're going to need help. And so, we created One Life at a Time, and the next chapter of my life began.

I opened One Life at a Time—a 501(c) (3) nonprofit—in November 2008 in response to the rise in unemployment and underemployment in the New England area and throughout the United States. I founded One Life at a Time to help people find employment and to find hope in their job search. Unless you have suffered a job loss or another profound loss, you cannot imagine what it is like to walk in that person's shoes. Losses are humbling experiences and sometimes crippling life changes. Sometimes your quality of life changes significantly, and the stress can be overwhelming for not only the job seeker but for the job seeker's family as well.

I can't stress enough to everyone I meet at One Life at a Time that it's OK to feel bad about a job loss. I even encourage people to vocalize those feelings. Then I ask, "OK, now what?" Sometimes that question surprises people. I don't say it to be insensitive, but to instill hope that better days are coming.

You have to believe that this temporary job loss is just that — temporary — and that you will eventually get your life back. When you're out of work, you have to work at finding new employment, and that may mean a great deal of adjustment. I remember that it was a difficult time, but with hard work, networking, and refocusing, I did reenter the workforce.

I can tell when people get it. They have a certain determination. They work hard, polish up their skills, and get back to work. In some instances, it may mean a job change.

Despite the alarming unemployment statistics we see in the media, I still see people finding meaningful employment. It may not always be their dream job at first, but it's meaningful enough to heal their prior job loss and move them toward their goals. It is really rewarding to see people pick themselves up and, after some hard work, get back to a paying job. It truly never gets old to see that joy in people when they have found work again.

The organization is all about making a difference, one life at a time. We help people update their resumes, computer skills, social media skills, and interviewing skills. And people are so appreciative of a facility that really sees them as individuals instead of numbers.

## Our Mission

At One Life at a Time, we pledge to help those in need of employment assistance and are committed to preparing our clients to rejoin the workforce. Our approach is to offer unique, compassionate, and effective solutions to our clients. We strive to help all of our clients reach their potential and find meaningful employment. Our job development specialists work hard to ensure our clients are given not only practical support but moral support as well. We understand that unemployment can be a difficult time, and we want to help our clients through this process.

## Early Beginnings

When One Life at a Time was born in 2008, we had three employees and occupied a small, three-room house in a suburb south of Boston, Massachusetts. By 2009, despite the high unemployment rate nationally and in our New England area, One Life at a Time had helped over 11,000 clients from diverse walks of life find jobs.

## One Life Today

Our workforce has grown from three employees to twelve, and we are most proud of two new Job Training Programs for our clients and the fact that we have helped over 11,000 clients find jobs. We have a success rate of 89% of individuals who enroll in the program are currently employed.

Our website www.1lifeatatime.org welcomes potential clients to learn more about whom we are, what we do, and our focus. We can also be found on Face book and Twitter.

We have a new two week Adult Job Training Program, a Young Adult Job Training Program. We also have Microsoft Office Certification Prep Classes and QuickBooks Certification Prep Program that have been approved by the Massachusetts Department of Education.

Whether you have a job and wish to improve your computer skills for a better or more fulfilling career choice, or are just learning, there are a lot of great training opportunities at One Life at a Time. We offer job assistance for the unemployed or underemployed. We have partnered with local businesses and community organizations in an effort to better understand their hiring needs and candidate requirements to fill positions with our program participants.

We are able to provide free career services aimed at empowering individuals at all professional and educational levels to actualize their potential and obtain what they need to be successful in the work place. We are currently looking for donors and grants who would like to contribute to the success of One Life at a Time.

One Life at a Time assists in coaching and mentoring adults with career-building essentials so they can obtain and retain gainful employment. Through these services, our job development specialists strive to instill a tangible hope to job seekers that they *can* take charge of their careers, even in uncertain times.

By learning about a company's hiring needs, we implement key strategies and resources to ensure individuals receive appropriate training to meet the demands of today's job marketplace.

**Resume and Cover Letter Preparation:** Career development specialists will give you the keys to successfully prepare and write a resume. They will help you display your experience, education, and training in the best possible manner to ensure that you will receive full and proper consideration and increase your chances of obtaining a job.

**Job Search Tactics and Trends:** Career development specialist will show you how and where you can begin searching for your ideal job. They will supply you with useful tools on how to post resumes with many of the major career networking websites and keep you notified of job fairs available in your area.

**Interview and Presentation Skills**: Job development specialists will schedule mock interviews to help improve your business communication skills and act appropriately with confidence in any situation.

**Relationship Building:** One Life staff members act as liaisons between employers they have partnered with and hopeful clients seeking employment, in an effort to match qualified job seekers with open positions.

**Networking Techniques**: At One Life, we stress the importance of networking in a job search.

**Social Media Training:** Job development specialists will provide assistance with social media, including LinkedIn. You will learn to create and update your LinkedIn profile.

**Job Placement Assistance**: Job development specialists will begin job searches based on your qualifications, notify you of any opportunities, advocate on your behalf, and transmit your resume on if the need should arise.

**Computer Training**: Computer specialists will offer tutorials in the following areas based on your specific needs: Microsoft Suite (Word, Excel, Outlook, PowerPoint, and Access); Microsoft Windows; web design with FrontPage; QuickBooks Pro; Typing Master Pro, Internet research, and e-mail (compose, send, and attachments).

Participants not only receive encouragement, support, ideas, and resources from the instructor but from peers as well. The program has been met with a great deal of support from our recent graduates.

Upon completion of the program, job placement assistance will be provided to the participants.

## Follow-Up with Job Development Specialists

After completing the three-week Job Ready Program, clients are encouraged to meet with a job development specialist to continue their job search. The importance of these post-workshop meetings is twofold: clients report the status of their job search and job development specialists contact employers in an effort to match qualified clients with open positions. Placement is our ultimate goal. Currently we place close to 80 percent of our clients.

Job development specialists also discuss with clients courses and post-workshop training that One Life offers to help improve their computer skills, revise their resume, or polish their job pitch.

## New Free Young Adult Job Ready Training Program

In July 2014 One Life was pleased to introduce a program specifically designed to help young adults find meaningful employment. Participants will learn how to utilize social media in their job search, how to present themselves professionally, how to fill out job applications and other forms, and more!

As an adult who received a degree later in life, I wanted these young students to understand how important goals and the desire to succeed were for me, and I hope to impart that through this program.

I feel a connection to them when I explain that I did not enter college when I graduated from high school, but through hard work and determination, I founded a medical lab business with nine thousand dollars in small, personal loans and sold the business a few years later for $1.5 million. That generally gets their attention.

I feel One Life has evolved in a really good way from our humble beginnings.

We additionally offer young adults help with transitioning out of foster care. We work with the local Department of Children and Families to help with getting them back to work and finding them housing. We also work with STARR programs run by Bay State Community Services to help younger teens develop the skills to enter the workforce; we also work with the foster youth aging out of the Foster Care system helping them find employment and housing.

## What's Ahead for One Life at a Time

I wish I had more resources and locations to help all that are unemployed or underemployed. My staff and I are optimistic despite the uncertainty of the job market we can help those that walk through our doors. I tell the clients that come to 'One Life at a Time' sometimes you have to take a job you are qualified for to pay the bills and work that dream job as a part time endeavor. A good analogy is the struggling actor whose day job is working a full time job and then moonlights as an actor part time.

I know from personal experience that the loss of a job and the lack of funds to support yourself can be a stressful time and devastating at times. I know firsthand the emotional toll unemployment can take.

I lost things and I could have lost everything, but I picked myself up and got back on my feet. I wanted to make sure that other people looking for jobs could have some resources to help with their job search.

I also know that having gone through some turbulent times, it's our relationships, our connections to God, family and friends that see us through the tough times. Personal relationships nurture us, comfort us, and bring meaning to our life each day.

## Friends of One Life at a Time

As a 501(c)(3) nonprofit organization designed and committed to providing personalized career services to individuals who are unemployed or underemployed, we rely on the generosity of Friends of One Life at a Time.

We have advertised locally and are proud to state that as of January we have helped over 11,400 individuals find employment.

Here is how you can give back.

**Donations**: We need the help of other business owners, foundations, and private donors to continue our mission. Our resources are limited; the needs of our clients are great. Please consider making a contribution or partnering with us.

Our organization has been seen on the *Nightly News with Brian Williams* and in articles in *The Patriot Ledger,* and *The Boston Globe*.

Your donation will help people pursue a better life through career development training and mentoring. They will receive *free*: career planning, computer training, skills assessments, resume preparation, interviewing skills, office etiquette training, image consultations, job search planning, and job placement assistance.

Donations will also help us build critical partnerships with local employers, which will allow us to find quality jobs for our clients. We invite you to make a tax-deductible donation to help us in our mission by either sending a check to One Life at a Time.

We thank you in advance for your contribution!

One Life at a Time
400 Washington Street,
Braintree, MA 02184
ph: 781.681.7003
www.1lifeatatime.org
Attention: Christine Driscoll-O'Neill

At times I thought I was alone. I realize now that God was carrying me.

Christine Driscoll-O'Neill